Cleveland Indians 2020

A Baseball Companion

Edited by R.J. Anderson, Craig Goldstein and Bret Sayre

Baseball Prospectus

Craig Brown, Steven Goldman and David Pease, Consultant Editors
Robert Au, Harry Pavlidis and Amy Pircher, Statistics Editors

Library of Congress Cataloging-in-Publication Data:
paperback
ISBN-13: 978-1-949332-70-4

Project Credits
Cover Design: Michael Byzewski at Aesthetic Apparatus
Interior Design and Production: Jeff Pease, Dave Pease
Layout: Jeff Pease, Dave Pease

Baseball icon courtesy of Uberux, from https://www.shareicon.net/author/uberux

Ballpark diagram courtesy of Lou Spirito/THIRTY81 Project, https://thirty81project.com/

Manufactured in the United States of America
10 9 8 7 6 5 4 3 2 1

Table of Contents

Statistical Introduction

Sports are, fundamentally, a blend of athletic endeavor and storytelling. Baseball, like any other sport, tells its stories in so many ways: in the arc of a game from the stands or a season from the box scores, in photos, or even in numbers. At Baseball Prospectus, we understand that statistics don't replace observation or any of baseball's stories, but complement everything else that makes the game so much fun.

What stats help us with is with patterns and precision, variance and value. This book can help you learn things you may not see from watching a game or hundred, whether it's the path of a career over time or the breadth of the entire MLB. We'd also never ask you to choose between our numbers and the experience of viewing a game from the cheap seats or the comfort of your home; our publication combines running the numbers with observations and wisdom from some of the brightest minds we can find. But if you *do* want to learn more about the numbers beyond what's on the backs of player jerseys, let us help explain.

Offense

We've revised our methodology for determining batting value. Long-time readers of the book will notice that we've retired True Average in favor of a new metric: Deserved Runs Created Plus (DRC+). Developed by Jonathan Judge and our stats team, this statistic measures everything a player does at the plate–reaching base, hitting for power, making outs, and moving runners over–and puts it on a scale where 100 equals league-average performance. A DRC+ of 150 is terrific, a DRC+ of 100 is average and a DRC+ of 75 means you better be an excellent defender.

DRC+ also does a better job than any of our previous metrics in taking contextual factors into account. The model adjusts for how the park affects performance, but also for things like the talent of the opposing pitcher, value of different types of batted-ball events, league, temperature and other factors. It's able to describe a player's expected offensive contribution than any other statistic we've found over the years, and also does a better job of predicting future performance as well.

There's a lot more to DRC+'s story, and you can read all about it in greater depth near the end of this book.

The other aspect of run-scoring is baserunning, which we quantify using Baserunning Runs. BRR not only records the value of stolen bases (or getting caught in the act), but also accounts for all the stuff that doesn't show up on the back of a baseball card: a runner's ability to go first to third on a single, or advance on a fly ball.

Defense

Where offensive value is *relatively* easy to identify and understand, defensive value is...not. Over the past dozen years, the sabermetric community has focused mostly on stats based on zone data: a real-live human person records the type of batted ball and estimated landing location, and models are created that give expected outs. From there, you can compare fielders' actual outs to those expected ones. Simple, right?

Unfortunately, zone data has two major issues. First, zone data is recorded by commercial data providers who keep the raw data private unless you pay for it. (All the statistics we build in this book and on our website use public data as inputs.) That hurts our ability to test assumptions or duplicate results. Second, over the years it has become apparent that there's quite a bit of "noise" in zone-based fielding analysis. Sometimes the conclusions drawn from zone data don't hold up to scrutiny, and sometimes the different data provided by different providers don't look anything alike, giving wildly different results. Sometimes the hard-working professional stringers or scorers might unknowingly inflict unconscious bias into the mix: for example good fielders will often be credited with more expected outs despite the data, and ballparks with high press boxes tend to score more line drives than ones with a lower press box.

Enter our Fielding Runs Above Average (FRAA). For most positions, FRAA is built from play-by-play data, which allows us to avoid the subjectivity found in many other fielding metrics. The idea is this: count how many fielding plays are made by a given player and compare that to expected plays for an average fielder at their position (based on pitcher ground ball tendencies and batter handedness). Then we adjust for park and base-out situations.

When it comes to catchers, our methodology is a little different thanks to the laundry list of responsibilities they're tasked with beyond just, well, catching and throwing the ball. By now you've probably heard about "framing" or the art of making umpires more likely to call balls outside the strike zone for strikes. To put this into one tidy number, we incorporate pitch tracking data (for the years it exists) and adjust for important factors like pitcher, umpire, batter and home-field advantage using a mixed-model approach. This grants us a number for how many strikes the catcher is personally adding to (or subtracting from) his pitchers' performance...which we then convert to runs added or lost using linear weights.

Framing is one of the biggest parts of determining catcher value, but we also take into account blocking balls from going past, whether a scorer deems it a passed ball or a wild pitch. We use a similar approach—one that really benefits from the pitch tracking data that tells us what ends up in the dirt and what doesn't. We also include a catcher's ability to prevent stolen bases and how well they field balls in play, and *finally* we come up with our FRAA for catchers.

Pitching

Both pitching and fielding make up the half of baseball that isn't run scoring: run prevention. Separating pitching from fielding is a tough task, and most recent pitching analysis has branched off from Voros McCracken's famous (and controversial) statement, "There is little if any difference among major-league pitchers in their ability to prevent hits on balls hit in the field of play." The research of the analytic community has validated this to some extent, and there are a host of "defense-independent" pitching measures that have been developed to try and extract the effect of the defense behind a hurler from the pitcher's work.

Our solution to this quandary is Deserved Run Average (DRA), our core pitching metric. DRA looks like earned run average (ERA), the tried-and-true pitching stat you've seen on every baseball broadcast or box score from the past century, but it's very different. To start, DRA takes an event-by-event look at what the pitchers does, and adjusts the value of that event based on different environmental factors like park, batter, catcher, umpire, base-out situation, run differential, inning, defense, home field advantage, pitcher role and temperature. That mixed model gives us a pitcher's expected contribution, similar to what we do for our DRC+ model for hitters and FRAA model for catchers. (Oh, and we also consider the pitcher's effect on basestealing and on balls getting past the catcher.)

It's important to note that DRA is set to the scale of runs allowed per nine innings (RA9) instead of ERA, which makes DRA's scale slightly higher than ERA's. The reason for this is because ERA tends to overrate three types of pitchers:

1. Pitchers who play in parks where scorers hand out more errors. Official scorers differ significantly in the frequency at which they assign errors to fielders.
2. Ground-ball pitchers, because a substantial proportion of errors occur on groundballs.
3. Pitchers who aren't very good. Better pitchers often allow fewer unearned runs than bad pitchers, because good pitchers tend to find ways to get out of jams.

Since the last time you picked up an edition of this book, we've also made a few minor changes to DRA to make it better. Recent research into "tunneling"—the act of throwing consecutive pitches that appear similar from a batter's point of view until after the swing decision point–data has given us a new contextual factor to account for in DRA: plate distance. This refers to the distance between successive pitches as they approach the plate, and while it has a smaller effect than factors like velocity or whiff rate, it still can help explain pitcher strikeout rate in our model.

New Pitching Metrics for 2020

We're including a few "new" pitching metrics in the book for the 2020 edition, though unlike last year, these numbers may be a little bit more familiar to those of you who have spent some time investigating baseball statistics.

Fastball Percentage

Our fastball percentage (FB%) statistic measures how frequently a pitcher throws a pitch classified as a "fastball," measured as a percentage of overall pitches thrown. We qualify three types of fastballs:

1. The traditional four-seam fastball;
2. The two-seam fastball or sinker;
3. "Hard cutters," which are pitches that have the movement profile of a cut fastball and are used as the pitcher's primary offering or in place of a more traditional fastball.

For example, a pitcher with a FB% of 67 throws any combination of these three pitches about two-thirds of the time.

Whiff Rate

Everybody loves a swing and a miss, and whiff rate (WHF) measures how frequently pitchers induce a swinging strike. To calculate WHF, we add up all the pitches thrown that ended with a swinging strike, then divide that number by a pitcher's total pitches thrown. Most often, high whiff rates correlate with high strikeout rates (and overall effective pitcher performance).

Called Strike Probability

Called Strike Probability (CSP) is a number that represents the likelihood that all of a pitcher's pitches will be called a strike while controlling for location, pitcher and batter handedness, umpire and count. Here's how it works: on each pitch, our model determines how many times (out of 100) that a similar pitch was called for a strike given those factors mentioned above, and when normalized for each batter's strike zone. Then we average the CSP for all pitches thrown by a pitcher in a season, and that gives us the yearly CSP percentage you see in the stats boxes.

As you might imagine, pitchers with a higher CSP are more likely to work in the zone, where pitchers with a lower CSP are likely locating their pitches outside the normal strike zone, for better or for worse.

Projections

Many of you aren't turning to this book just for a look at what a player has done, but for a look at what a player is going to do: the PECOTA projections. PECOTA, initially developed by Nate Silver (who has moved on to greater fame as a political analyst), consists of three parts:

1. Major-league equivalencies, which use minor-league statistics to project how a player will perform in the major leagues;
2. Baseline forecasts, which use weighted averages and regression to the mean to estimate a player's current true talent level; and
3. Aging curves, which uses the career paths of comparable players to estimate how a player's statistics are likely to change over time.

With all those important things covered, let's take a look at what's in the book this year.

Team Prospectus

Most of this book is composed of team chapters, with one for each of the 30 major-league franchises. On the first page of each chapter, you'll see a box that contains some of the key statistics for each team as well as a very inviting stadium diagram. (You can see an example of this for the Milwaukee Brewers on this very page!)

We start with the team name, their unadjusted 2019 win-loss record, and their divisional ranking. Beneath that are a host of other team statistics. **Pythag** presents an adjusted 2019 winning percentage, calculated by taking runs scored per game (**RS/G**) and runs allowed per game (**RA/G**) for the team, and running them through a version of Bill James' Pythagorean formula that was refined and improved by David Smyth and Brandon Heipp. (The formula is called "Pythagenpat," which is equally fun to type and to say.)

Next up is **DRC+**, described earlier, to indicate the overall hitting ability of the team either above or below league-average. Run prevention on the pitching side is covered by **DRA** (also mentioned earlier) and another metric: Fielding Independent Pitching (**FIP**), which calculates another ERA-like statistic based on strikeouts, walks, and home runs recorded. Defensive Efficiency Rating (**DER**) tells us the percentage of balls in play turned into outs for the team, and is a quick fielding shorthand that rounds out run prevention.

After that, we have several measures related to roster composition, as opposed to on-field performance. **B-Age** and **P-Age** tell us the average age of a team's batters and pitchers, respectively. **Salary** is the combined team payroll for all on-field players, and Doug Pappas' Marginal Dollars per Marginal Win (**M$/MW**) tells us how much money a team spent to earn production above replacement level.

Ending this batch of statistics is the number of disabled list days a team had over the season (**IL Days**) and the amount of salary paid to players on the disabled list (**$ on IL**); this final number is expressed as a percentage of total payroll.

Next to each of these stats, we've listed each team's MLB rank in that category from first to 30th. In this, first always indicates a positive outcome and 30th a negative outcome, except in the case of salary—first is highest.

After the franchise statistics, we share a few items about the team's home ballpark. There's the aforementioned diagram of the park's dimensions (including distances to the outfield wall), a graphic showing the height of the wall from the left-field pole to the right-field pole, and a table showing three-year park factors for the stadium. The park factors are displayed as indexes where 100 is average, 110 means that the park inflates the statistic in question by 10 percent, and 90 means that the park deflates the statistic in question by 10 percent.

On the second page of each team chapter, you'll find three graphs. The first is the **2019 Hit List Ranking**. This shows our Hit List Rank for the team on each day of the 2019 season and is intended to give you a picture of the ups and downs of the team's season. Hit List Rank measures overall team performance and drives the Hit List Power Rankings at the baseballprospectus.com website.

The second graph is **Committed Payroll** and helps you see how the team's payroll has compared to the MLB and divisional average payrolls over time. Payroll figures are current as of January 1, 2020; with so many free agents still unsigned as of this writing, the final 2020 figure will likely be significantly different for many teams. (In the meantime, you can always find the most current data at Baseball Prospectus' Cot's Baseball Contracts page.)

The third graph is **Farm System Ranking** and displays how the Baseball Prospectus prospect team has ranked the organization's farm system since 2007.

After the graphs, we have a **Personnel** section that lists many of the important decision-makers and upper-level field and operations staff members for the franchise, as well as any former Baseball Prospectus staff members who are currently part of the organization. (In very rare circumstances, someone might be on both lists!)

Juan Soto LF

Born: 10/25/98 Age: 21 Bats: L Throws: L
Height: 6'1" Weight: 185 Origin: International Free Agent, 2015

YEAR	TEAM	LVL	AGE	PA	R	2B	3B	HR	RBI	BB	K	SB	CS	AVG/OBP/SLG
2017	NAT	RK	18	27	3	1	1	0	4	2	1	0	0	.320/.370/.440
2017	HAG	A	18	96	15	5	0	3	14	10	8	1	2	.360/.427/.523
2018	HAG	A	19	74	12	5	3	5	24	14	13	2	0	.373/.486/.814
2018	POT	A+	19	73	17	3	1	7	18	11	8	0	1	.371/.466/.790
2018	HAR	AA	19	35	4	2	0	2	10	4	7	1	0	.323/.400/.581
2018	WAS	MLB	19	494	77	25	1	22	70	79	99	5	2	.292/.406/.517
2019	WAS	MLB	20	659	110	32	5	34	110	108	132	12	1	.282/.401/.548
2020	WAS	MLB	21	630	92	30	3	35	102	85	123	5	2	.284/.382/.543

Comparables: Ronald Acuña Jr., Mike Trout, Tony Conigliaro

YEAR	TEAM	LVL	AGE	PA	DRC+	VORP	BABIP	BRR	FRAA	WARP
2017	NAT	RK	18	27	135	1.5	.333	0.0	RF(9): -1.1	0.0
2017	HAG	A	18	96	181	8.0	.373	1.0	RF(19): -1.9, LF(2): -0.3	0.9
2018	HAG	A	19	74	222	14.5	.405	0.3	RF(14): 1.1, CF(2): 0.2	1.2
2018	POT	A+	19	73	260	15.4	.340	1.4	RF(14): 1.0, LF(1): 0.0	1.6
2018	HAR	AA	19	35	113	3.6	.364	0.0	LF(4): 0.6, RF(4): -0.5	0.1
2018	WAS	MLB	19	494	125	40.5	.338	-0.5	LF(114): 2.7	3.0
2019	WAS	MLB	20	659	136	49.0	.312	1.4	LF(150): -0.8	4.9
2020	WAS	MLB	21	630	133	43.6	.310	-0.1	LF 3	4.8

Position Players

After all that information and a thoughtful bylined essay covering each team, we present our player comments. These are also bylined, but due to frequent franchise shifts during the offseason, our bylines are more a rough guide than a perfect accounting of who wrote what.

Each player is listed with the major-league team that employed him as of early January 2020. If a player changed teams after that point via free agency, trade, or any other method, you'll be able to find them in the chapter for their previous squad.

As an example, take a look at the player comment for Nationals outfielder Juan Soto: the stat block that accompanies his written comment is at the top of this page. First we cover biographical information (age is as of June 30, 2020) before moving onto the stats themselves. Our statistic columns include standard identifying information like **YEAR**, **TEAM**, **LVL** (level of affiliated play) and **AGE** before getting into the numbers. Next, we provide raw, untranslated numbers like you might find on the back of your dad's baseball cards: **PA** (plate appearances), **R** (runs), **2B** (doubles), **3B** (triples), **HR** (home runs), **RBI** (runs batted in), **BB** (walks), **K** (strikeouts), **SB** (stolen bases) and **CS** (caught stealing).

Next, we have unadjusted "slash" statistics: **AVG** (batting average), **OBP** (on-base percentage) and **SLG** (slugging percentage). Following the slash line is **DRC+** (Deserved Runs Created Plus), which we described earlier as total offensive expected contribution compared to the league average.

One of our oldest active metrics, **VORP** (Value Over Replacement Player), considers offensive production, position and plate appearances. In essence, it is the number of runs contributed beyond what a replacement-level player at the same position would contribute if given the same percentage of team plate appearances. VORP does not consider the quality of a player's defense.

BABIP (batting average on balls in play) tells us how often a ball in play fell for a hit, and can help us identify whether a batter may have been lucky or not...but note that high BABIPs also tend to follow the great hitters of our time, as well as speedy singles hitters who put the ball on the ground.

The next item is **BRR** (Baserunning Runs), which covers all of a player's baserunning accomplishments including (but not limited to) swiped bags and failed attempts. Next is **FRAA** (Fielding Runs Above Average), which also includes the number of games previously played at each position noted in parentheses. Multi-position players have only their two most frequent positions listed here, but their total FRAA number reflects all positions played.

Our last column here is **WARP** (Wins Above Replacement Player). WARP estimates the total value of a player, which means for hitters it takes into account hitting runs above average (calculated using the DRC+ model), BRR and FRAA. Then, it makes an adjustment for positions played and gives the player a credit for plate appearances based upon the difference between "replacement level"—which is derived from the quality of players added to a team's roster after the start of the season–and the league average.

The final line just below the stats box is **PECOTA** data, which is discussed further in a following section.

Catchers

Catchers are a special breed, and thus they have earned their own separate box which displays some of the defensive metrics that we've built just for them. As an example, let's check out J.T. Realmuto.

The **YEAR** and **TEAM** columns match what you'd find in the other stat box. **P. COUNT** indicates the number of pitches thrown while the catcher was behind the plate, including swinging strikes, fouls and balls in play. **FRM RUNS** is the total run value the catcher provided (or cost) his team by influencing the umpire to call strikes where other catchers did not. **BLK RUNS** expresses the total run value above or below average for the catcher's ability to prevent wild pitches and passed balls. **THRW RUNS** is calculated using a similar model as the previous two statistics, and it measures a catcher's ability to throw out basestealers but also to dissuade them from testing his arm in the first place. It takes into account factors like the pitcher (including his delivery and pickoff move) and baserunner (who could be as fast as Billy Hamilton or as slow as Yonder Alonso). **TOT RUNS** is the sum of all of the previous three statistics.

Justin Verlander   RHP

Born: 02/20/83   Age: 37   Bats: R   Throws: R
Height: 6'5"   Weight: 225   Origin: Round 1, 2004 Draft (#2 overall)

YEAR	TEAM	LVL	AGE	W	L	SV	G	GS	IP	H	HR	BB/9	K/9	K	GB%	BABIP
2017	DET	MLB	34	10	8	0	28	28	172	153	23	3.5	9.2	176	34%	.283
2017	HOU	MLB	34	5	0	0	5	5	34	17	4	1.3	11.4	43	32%	.194
2018	HOU	MLB	35	16	9	0	34	34	214	156	28	1.6	12.2	290	31%	.272
2019	HOU	MLB	36	21	6	0	34	34	223	137	36	1.7	12.1	300	36%	.219
2020	HOU	MLB	37	15	6	0	29	29	184	138	28	2.3	12.1	248	35%	.274

Comparables: Zack Greinke, A.J. Burnett, Aníbal Sánchez

YEAR	TEAM	LVL	AGE	WHIP	ERA	DRA	WARP	MPH	FB%	WHF	CSP
2017	DET	MLB	34	1.28	3.82	4.03	3.0	97.7	58	11	47.8
2017	HOU	MLB	34	0.65	1.06	3.08	0.9	97.5	59.6	15.1	49.9
2018	HOU	MLB	35	0.90	2.52	2.33	7.3	97.5	61.2	16.2	51.6
2019	HOU	MLB	36	0.80	2.58	2.51	7.9	96.8	49.9	17.5	48.3
2020	HOU	MLB	37	1.01	2.75	2.95	5.3	95.8	54.6	15.1	48.2

Pitchers

Let's give our pitchers a turn, using 2019 AL Cy Young winner Justin Verlander as our example. Take a look at his stat block: the first line and the **YEAR**, **TEAM**, **LVL** and **AGE** columns are the same as in the position player example earlier.

Here too, we have a series of columns that display raw, unadjusted statistics compiled by the pitcher over the course of a season: **W** (wins), **L** (losses), **SV** (saves), **G** (games pitched), **GS** (games started), **IP** (innings pitched), **H** (hits allowed) and **HR** (home runs allowed). Next we have two statistics that are rates: **BB/9** (walks per nine innings) and **K/9** (strikeouts per nine innings), before returning to the unadjusted K (strikeouts).

Next up is **GB%** (ground ball percentage), which is the percentage of all batted balls that were hit on the ground, including both outs and hits. Remember, this is based on observational data and subject to human error, so please approach this with a healthy dose of skepticism.

BABIP (batting average on balls in play) is calculated using the same methodology as it is for position players, but it often tells us more about a pitcher than it does a hitter. With pitchers, a high BABIP is often due to poor defense or bad luck, and can often be an indicator of potential rebound, and a low BABIP may be cause to expect performance regression. (A typical league-average BABIP is close to .290-.300.)

The metrics **WHIP** (walks plus hits per inning pitched) and **ERA** (earned run average) are old standbys: WHIP measures walks and hits allowed on a per-inning basis, while ERA measures earned runs on a nine-inning basis. Neither of these stats are translated or adjusted.

DRA (Deserved Run Average) was described at length earlier, and measures how many runs the pitcher "deserved" to allow per nine innings. Please note that since we lack all the data points that would make for a "real" DRA for minor-league events, the DRA displayed for minor league partial-seasons is based off of different data. (That data is a modified version of our cFIP metric, which you can find more information about on our website.)

Just like with hitters, **WARP** (Wins Above Replacement Player) is a total value metric that puts pitchers of all stripes on the same scale as position players. We use DRA as the primary input for our calculation of WARP. You might notice that relief pitchers (due to their limited innings) may have a lower WARP than you were expecting or than you might see in other WARP-like metrics. WARP does not take leverage into account, just the actions a pitcher performs and the expected value of those actions...which ends up judging high-leverage relief pitchers differently than you might imagine given their prestige and market value.

MPH gives you the pitcher's 95th percentile velocity for the noted season, in order to give you an idea of what the *peak* fastball velocity a pitcher possesses. Since this comes from our pitch-tracking data, it is not publicly available for minor-league pitchers.

Finally, we display the three new pitching metrics we described earlier. **FB%** (fastball percentage) gives you the percentage of fastballs thrown out of all pitches. **WHF** (whiff rate) tells you the percentage of swinging strikes induced out of all pitches. **CSP** (called strike probability) expresses the likelihood of all pitches thrown to result in a called strike, after controlling for factors like handedness, umpire, pitch type, count and location.

PECOTA

All players have PECOTA projections for 2020, as well as a set of other numbers that describe the performance of comparable players according to PECOTA. All projections for 2020 are for the player at the date we went to press in early January and are projected into the league and park context as indicated by the team abbreviation. (Note that players at very low levels of the minors are too unpredictable to assess using these numbers.) All PECOTA projected statistics represent a player's projected major-league performance.

Below the projections are the player's three highest-scoring comparable players as determined by PECOTA. All comparables represent a snapshot of how the listed player was performing at the same age as the current player, so if a

23-year-old pitcher is compared to Bartolo Colón, he's actually being compared to a 23-year-old Colón, not the version that pitched for the Rangers in 2018, nor to Colón's career as a whole.

A few points about pitcher projections. First, we aren't yet projecting peak velocity, so that column will be blank in the PECOTA lines. Second, projecting DRA is trickier than evaluating past performance, because it is unclear how deserving each pitcher will be of his anticipated outcomes. However, we know that another DRA-related statistic–contextual FIP or cFIP-estimates future run scoring very well. So for PECOTA, the projected DRA figures you see are based on the past cFIPs generated by the pitcher and comparable players over time, along with the other factors described above.

Lineouts

In each chapter's Lineouts section, you'll find abbreviated text comments, as well as all the same information you'd find in our full player comments. The only difference is that we limit the stats boxes in this section to only including the 2019 information for each player.

Managers

After all those wonderful team chapters, we've got statistics for each big-league manager, all of whom are organized by alphabetical order. Here you'll find a block including an extraordinary amount of information collected from each manager's entire career. For more information on the acronyms and what they mean, please visit the Glossary at www.baseballprospectus.com.

There is one important metric that we'd like to call attention to, and you'll find it next to each manager's name: **wRM+** (weighted reliever management plus). Developed by Rob Arthur and Rian Watt, wRM+ investigates how good a manager is at using their best relievers during the moments of highest leverage, using both our proprietary DRA metric as well as Leverage Index. wRM+ is scaled to a league average of 100, and a wRM+ of 105 indicates that relievers were used approximately five percent "better" than average. On the other hand, a wRM+ of 95 would tell us the team used its relievers five percent "worse" than the average team.

While wRM+ does not have an extremely strong correlation with a manager, it is statistically significant; this means that a manager is not *entirely* responsible for a team's wRM+, but does have some effect on that number.

PECOTA Leaderboards

If you're familiar with PECOTA, then you'll have noticed that the projection system often appears bullish on players coming off a bad year and bearish on players coming off a good year. (This is because the system weights several previous seasons, not just the most recent one.) In addition, we publish the 50th percentile projections for each player–which is smack in the middle of the range of projected production—which tends to mean PECOTA stat lines don't often have extreme results like 40 home runs or 250 strikeouts in a given season. In essence, PECOTA doesn't project very many extreme seasons.

At the end of the book, we've ranked the top players at each position based on their PECOTA projections. This might help you visualize just how a given player's projection compares to that of their peers, so that even if a dramatic stat line isn't projected, you can still imagine how they stack up against the rest of the league.

Part 1: Team Analysis

Cleveland Indians: Where Are You Going, Where Have You Been?

Collin Whitchurch, Jeffrey Paternostro and Matthew Trueblood

2019: What Went Right

Cleveland entered the season embracing the stars-and-scrubs mantra in a more extreme fashion than perhaps any team in baseball. Francisco Lindor, José Ramirez, Corey Kluber, Carlos Carrasco, and Brad Hand were all among the best at their respective positions in the game. It was the other pieces who were supposed to make or break their season.

Many of those auxiliary parts excelled, none more than 1B/DH Carlos Santana, who returned after a brief sabbatical in Philadelphia and put up the best season of his career in his age-33 season. Santana paired his trademark consistency in playing time (152 or more games played for the seventh straight year) and patience (OBP near .400 and as many walks as strikeouts) with career-best marks in home runs, OPS, DRC+, and WARP. He was the one staple in a lineup that suffered from injuries and roster turnover throughout the season.

Santana wasn't the only veteran to emerge. Roberto Pérez was handed regular playing time for the first time in his career in his age-30 season and socked 24 home runs after accumulating 21 in total through the first five years of his career. He was an above-average offensive catcher and the best defensive catcher in the American League—a rare combination in today's game.

It wasn't all old guys. Oscar Mercado, acquired in a minor deal with the Cardinals a year ago, was promoted in mid-May and secured the center field job with a solid rookie season while Jordan Luplow emerged from a meh mish-mash of outfielders to provide good production in a platoon role (.320/.439/.742 in 155 plate appearances against left-handed pitching). Then there was, of course, the blockbuster deadline acquisitions of Yasiel Puig and Franmil Reyes. The former locked down right field in his walk year while the latter provided a boost at DH. Both posted a DRC+ above 100 during their time in Cleveland, even if they weren't game-changers.

On the pitching side, Cleveland saw moundsmen considered on the fringe entering the season emerge as potential long-term assets. Shane Bieber was considered a command/control, low-ceiling guy in the minors, but followed up his solid half-season debut in 2018 with an All-Star season and was the Tribe's one constant in a rotation that dealt with a litany of injuries. He was a five-win player, tossing more than 200 innings with a 3.68 DRA and the third-best K/BB rate in the American League.

Mike Clevinger pitched like an ace when he was healthy, Aaron Civale looked like a solid rotation piece in 10 starts (although his 5.13 DRA argues he was quite lucky), and while Carrasco didn't put up great numbers in 79 innings, being able to come back after being diagnosed with leukemia doesn't belong anywhere other than the "What Went Right" section.

2019: What Went Wrong

Expectations shape perceptions. The Cleveland Indians won 93 games in 2019, yet you'd be hard-pressed to find anyone willing to call it a successful campaign. They missed the playoffs for the first time since 2015. Cleveland approached 2019 like a bored high school student running out the clock on their senior year. It's not even that they didn't do the work, they didn't even go to school and skipped finals to do whip-its with their friends behind the 7/11.

Some of the shortfall was bad fortune, to be sure. Cleveland won only 91 games in 2018 and won the division by 13 games. The Twins won 101 games this year. What are you gonna do? For Cleveland the answer starts with what they *didn't* do. Instead of solidifying their hold on a division they had dominated for the better part of the last half-decade, management began worrying about the bottom line. They let Michael Brantley and Andrew Miller walk, traded Yan Gomes for salary relief, and were content entering the season with the fading Jason Kipnis at second base and a bunch of AI-generated players from "MLB The Show" polluting the outfield.

That's all fine and dandy when you have a two-time Cy Young winner anchoring your rotation and a pair of fire-breathing dragons standing on the left side of the infield, but the universe laughs at the plans of generals and baseball teams. Lindor had a fine season, but by the high standards he'd established played more like a solid regular than a MVP contender. Ramirez had a nightmarish first half in which he produced .218/.308/.344. He finally turned back into the Ramirez from 2017-18 in the second half, but then missed a month with fractured right hamate bone. Kluber broke his arm at the beginning of May and never returned. In the seven starts he made before that, Kluber looked like an older, buggy model of the Klubot Cleveland had come to rely on. He was traded to the Rangers in December for a modest return.

The fringes of the roster weren't all sunshine and roses, either. The team gave 381 combined plate appearances to Leonys Martin and Carlos Gonzalez before putting them out to pasture. Tyler Naquin was good when he was healthy, but again couldn't stay on the field. Kipnis looked completely washed up. The depth pieces needed to pick up the slack when the stars were hurt—Mike Freeman, Yu Chang, Zach Plesac, et al—were unequal to the task. Hand continued to post his lofty strikeout totals but had a rough second half and lost the closer's job for a time. The rest of the bullpen collectively merits a shrug. Trevor Bauer couldn't replicate his Cy Young-caliber 2018 season, although trading him probably belongs in the first section given everything that accompanied him off the field.

Stars-and-scrubs is a winnable strategy when your stars play like stars. Cleveland did just fine employing that strategy the last few years, but ownership decided its pocketbook was more important than solidifying its position atop the AL Central mountain and a lack of depth—along with the Twins' improvement—reared its ugly head too many times to overcome. Whatever credit you give them for looking to patch those holes at the deadline is negated by their complete laissez faire approach to the offseason. They gambled that doing too little would be enough and got 93 wins. That's not a bad return on complacency, but nevertheless they deservedly sat out October. –*Collin Whitchurch*

Prospect Outlook

Cleveland is weird, man. I was half-tempted to kick off this section talking about **James Karinchak**, who is a reliever, albeit an extremely fun one. Instead let's chat about **Aaron Civale**, who went from "Shane-Bieber-lite" as a prospect to, "50 innings of 2018 Jacob deGrom," as a pro. The underlying stats don't support the shiny ERA, but Cleveland has had repeated success with this type of arm and Civale has done a fine job keeping the ball in the park so far despite the rabbit-ball era. At worst he looks like a useful number-four starter going forward. **Zach Plesac** didn't even have Civale's profile as a prospect, but has been a useful number-four starter himself, although I'm less confident that holds up another time through the league.

Getting those kinds of performances out of more marginal prospects was a boon for Cleveland, which has an improving system, but one where most of the talent is concentrated in the low minors. **Yu Chang** and **Bobby Bradley** scuffled in major league debuts while playing more or less to the scouting report in Triple-A, and pitcher **Triston McKenzie** missed all of 2019 with back issues, making third baseman **Nolan Jones** the most notable upper minors name. Jones had a fine 2019 campaign although there remain questions around both his ultimate defensive home and how much power he will get into games.

Beyond those two, most of the talent was concentrated in a loaded Mahoning Valley Penn League team that included outfielder **George Valera**, infielder **Brayan Rocchio**, and pitchers **Ethan Hankins** and **Carlos Vargas**. They also got an intriguing prep arm in the first round of the draft in **Daniel Espino**, but this cohort of players is—at a minimum—three years away from having an impact on the major league roster. —*Jeffrey Paternostro*

2020 Outlook

Teams that refuse to pay for premium free-agent talent, or pass on chances to trade big prospect value in exchange for an available star, are fond of telling fans to hold every season sacred—to think, as the team is supposedly trying to, of the years that come after this one, and after the next one. In life, it's good advice, and we should all embrace it a bit more consistently. In entertainment, it's dubious and we should all be suspicious of it. It's often cover for penurious owners who don't want to risk an extra $10 million in the pursuit of a trophy here or there—that is, to entertain you with a wholly-formed product. We should hold teams who say that to a corollary standard: every offseason is sacred, too.

MLB Network doesn't click off and air a test signal as soon as the World Series is over. Teams spend the fall and winter pleading with fans to buy season ticket packages, give season ticket packages as gifts, divide season ticket packages between friends, upgrade to premium season ticket packages, use season ticket packages as extra rolling paper in states with newly-passed marijuana laws going into effect. They hype jerseys and hats and spring training travel packages all winter. They stay in our pockets all year. It's fair, and perhaps even vital, for us to start expecting that they also provide a bit more of a year-round product.

The Indians were one of four teams who all but announced, at the dawn of the offseason, that their winter would be defined by the threat of Francisco Lindor being traded. They didn't even pay lip-service to the idea of building upon a championship-caliber core, of spending into the top half of the league in 2020 payroll, in order to take back what the Twins stole from them in 2019. They traded Kluber in mid-December, for a high-ceiling but cost-controlled reliever and a spare outfielder. That trade made plenty of sense; Kluber would only be the third-best starter for the 2020 Tribe. In context, however, it hit Cleveland fans like a concession.

The team signed César Hernández as a replacement for the departing Kipnis. That was a solid addition, too, even if Hernández seems a year past his days as an average regular. In context, however, it felt more like aiming low. They swapped backup catchers with the Red Sox, a two-step maneuver so patently meaningless and performative that it felt like a breaking of the fourth wall. Yes, both teams announced, as Kevin Plawecki drifted to Boston and Sandy Leon landed in Cleveland, we are sitting this winter out, unless we decide to trade your favorite player. Here's a bone; go sit in the corner and gnaw on it.

The 2020 Indians are going to be a pretty good team. If they find their fans' enthusiasm (or attendance) surprisingly lacking, though, they have only themselves to blame. They should remember better that their fans don't turn back into bank account numbers each November and that they'd engage them much better if they offered them more reasons to care. —*Matthew Trueblood*

Performance Graphs

2019 Hit List Ranking

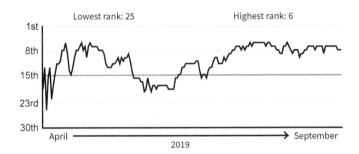

Committed Payroll (in millions)

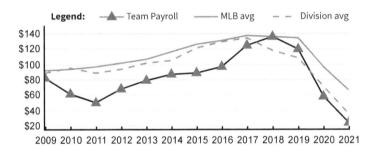

Farm System Ranking

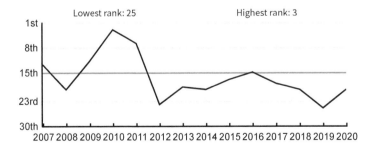

9

2019 Team Performance

ACTUAL STANDINGS

Team	W	L	Pct
MIN	101	61	0.623
CLE	**93**	**69**	**0.574**
CHA	72	89	0.447
KCA	59	103	0.364
DET	47	114	0.292

THIRD-ORDER STANDINGS

Team	W	L	Pct
MIN	97	65	0.597
CLE	**87**	**75**	**0.535**
CHA	66	95	0.412
KCA	59	103	0.364
DET	49	112	0.304

TOP HITTERS

Player	WARP
Carlos Santana	4.8
Roberto Pérez	4.7
Francisco Lindor	3.8

TOP PITCHERS

Player	WARP
Shane Bieber	4.9
Mike Clevinger	3.3
Trevor Bauer	1.9

VITAL STATISTICS

Statistic Name	Value	Rank
Pythagenpat	.573	8th
Runs Scored per Game	4.75	15th
Runs Allowed per Game	4.06	4th
Deserved Runs Created Plus	100	10th
Deserved Run Average	5.16	21st
Fielding Independent Pitching	4.09	7th
Defensive Efficiency Rating	.709	10th
Batter Age	27.8	12th
Pitcher Age	27.8	11th
Salary	$119.6M	19th
Marginal $ per Marginal Win	$2.4M	26th
Injured List Days	1066	16th
$ on IL	22%	23rd

2020 Team Projections

PROJECTED STANDINGS

Team	W	L	Pct	+/-
MIN	93.4	68.6	0.577	-8
CLE	**86.1**	**75.9**	**0.531**	**-7**
CHA	82.5	79.5	0.509	10
DET	69.2	92.8	0.427	22
KCA	67.8	94.2	0.419	9

TOP PROJECTED HITTERS

Player	WARP
Francisco Lindor	3.8
Roberto Pérez	3.7
Carlos Santana	3.3

TOP PROJECTED PITCHERS

Player	WARP
Shane Bieber	3.8
Mike Clevinger	2.6
Carlos Carrasco	2.5

FARM SYSTEM REPORT

Top Prospect	Number of Top 101 Prospects
George Valera, #58	4

KEY DEDUCTIONS

Player	WARP
Corey Kluber	2.4
Kevin Plawecki	0.6
Nick Goody	0.5
Tyler Clippard	0.4
Jason Kipnis	0.1
Cody Anderson	0.1
Andrew Velazquez	0.0
Eric Haase	-0.2

KEY ADDITIONS

Player	WARP
César Hernández	1.8
Delino DeShields	0.8
Domingo Santana	0.4
Daniel Johnson	0.2
Triston McKenzie	0.2
Beau Taylor	0.1
Emmanuel Clase	0.1
Sandy León	0.0
Scott Moss	0.0

Team Personnel

President, Baseball Operations
Chris Antonetti

General Manager
Mike Chernoff

Assistant General Manager
Carter Hawkins

Assistant General Manager
Matt Forman

Assistant General Manager
Sky Andrecheck

Manager
Terry Francona

BP Alumni
Max Marchi
Ethan Purser
Keith Woolner

Progressive Field Stats

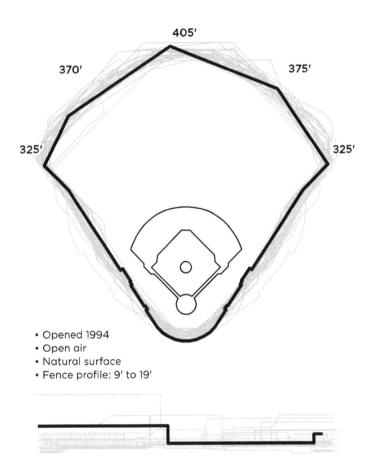

405'

370'   375'

325'   325'

- Opened 1994
- Open air
- Natural surface
- Fence profile: 9' to 19'

Three-Year Park Factors

Runs	Runs/RH	Runs/LH	HR/RH	HR/LH
101	99	105	99	104

Indians Team Analysis

If we're going to talk about the Indians, the legend of Sisyphus seems like as good a place to start as any. You probably know the basic outline: Dude has to push a very big rock up a hill for eternity; when he gets close to the top, the rock rolls to the bottom and he has to start all over again.

In the broad strokes, as a metaphor for Cleveland's legacy of title-free competitiveness goes, it isn't particularly tortured. But when you drill down to the original root of the legend, Sisyphus was being punished for being crafty and deceitful, greedy beyond avarice, controlling and murderous, opaque and ingenuine about his motives. In death, the rolling stone was Zeus's eternal punishment for how Sisyphus had used these qualities in life.

Looking at their recent run of competitiveness, you can understand a certain sense of frustration in this vein. They've averaged 91 wins per season over the last seven years, all of them above-.500 campaigns, winning three AL Central titles and a league pennant. That hardly seems like cause for celebration after a year in which they took their 93-win season straight to the links, no later than the epically awful Tigers or Royals. Heck, during that same seven-year stretch, the Royals—Ned Yost's Royals!—won a World Series.

Perhaps the most frustrating thing about 2019 was the sense that a window—of opportunity, to contend and to win with a roster built around Francisco Lindor—is closing. Some of that might be the product of recognizing that the Twins' agglomeration of talent is finally reaching critical mass at a time when Minnesota's profiting from smart management. Some of that may also be fear that something similar is on the way from the White Sox. The Age of Lindor in the Land, with just two years left to tick down before the star shortstop heads into free agency with a chance to make Harper or Machado money, is already clouded over.

Exacerbating that sense of frustration was the front office's failure to add anything approaching adequate outfield help last winter, effectively frittering away a Lindor-enabled season with division rivals on the rise. But to be fair, the decade just ending saw the Giants win three titles with strong starting pitching and cobbled-together outfields. Knowing that Oscar Mercado was on the way up, can you blame the Indians for giving that a shot last year after letting Michael Brantley walk away?

We can and should, of course, especially in light of their modest in-season trade for outfield reinforcements—with a strategically precise Trevor Bauer-ectomy, no less. Failing to give Brantley a qualifying offer was the big mistake; failing to get anyone in the vicinity of his value multiplied it. But, in fairness, let's remember that Franmil Reyes and Yasiel Puig didn't really outperform the Tyler Naquins or Jordan Luplows of the world. The problem wasn't quantitative as much as it was qualitative—the failure to acquire a premium outfield asset, Brantley-level or better—and evaluative, because Leonys Martín and Jake Bauers and Greg Allen didn't come close to cutting it, not in any offensive role.

Admittedly, getting players Brantley-grade good isn't easy. On the open market those guys can usually choose their own employers, and in trade they generally don't come cheap. Failing to get Brantley while—again—seeing Jason Kipnis continue to crumble and José Ramírez get off to a slow start exacerbated the sense that the Indians had been reduced to Frankie Lindor and the Smilettes. And the failure to adequately anticipate the scale of the problem bodes ill for a long-term future that may not have Lindor in it.

Getting 93 wins out of this roster despite Corey Kluber's injury or Carlos Carrasco's cancer or Ramírez's slow start might sound like a tremendous, brag-worthy accomplishment. It isn't. It's a Lindor year wasted. With just two of those left, Cleveland should consider the 2019 season a disaster.

Consider the value Lindor represents. Among shortstops through their age-25 seasons, Lindor ranks fifth all-time in WARP:

Shortstop	PA	WARP	Years in the Postseason
Alex Rodriguez	4247	40.2	3
Cal Ripken	3562	29.7	1 (won WS)
Francisco Lindor	3244	25.1	3 (lost WS x1)
Arky Vaughan	3712	24.0	0
Jim Fregosi	3487	21.0	0
Hanley Ramirez	2753	20.6	0
Robin Yount	4553	20.5	1
Nomar Garciaparra	2074	20.3	2
Troy Tulowitzki	2368	19.3	2 (lost WS x1)
Chris Speier	3086	17.9	1

The lone guy in the top five who never got as much as a pennant was Fregosi, whose career was a byword for tough luck. (Ramirez, Garciaparra and Speier join him when the bottom half of the list is considered.) Expand the scope to the top 20 and we can note that Derek Jeter won yet another title in his age-26 season, while Yount and Joe Cronin won AL pennants in theirs. Lou Boudreau, whose career predated free agency, would ultimately win the World Series. And on that note, by his age-26 season A-Rod was in his second season of cashing checks from the Rangers after his record-setting deal for a quarter of a billion dollars.

Other notables in the top 20 include Xander Bogaerts, José Reyes and Carlos Correa—franchise players, in short, who powered postseason runs very early on in their careers.

The lesson, as far as it goes, is that you're supposed to build around players of this caliber, not cash them in for prospects' prospects. So the proposition that the Indians might flip Frankie Lindor for prospects, at a time when the industry is historically reticent to yield value, would be historically remarkable, and downright disappointing almost any way you look at it.

In this particular pageant, nobody cares or should care about who wins Ms. Sabermetrically Savvy, even when the competition for it is fierce. It isn't the Indians who are on Sisyphus' eternal hamster wheel; their fans are, telling themselves stories about Andrew Miller or Rajai Davis or José Mesa or the Curse of Rocky Colavito or even Willie Mays if they can remember the heartbreak of the 1954 World Series. Terry Francona wouldn't be the first manager in Indians history to never put up a losing season without winning a World Series title, just the most famous since Al Lopez.[1]

Trading Bauer and subsequently Corey Kluber represent choices to convert the perishability of pitching prowess into future value (and rid themselves of the dubious charms of Bauer's insufferable *je ne sais quoi* while they were at it). There's a measure of irony in dispensing with both pitchers within a few months of one another; they have been held up as very different exemplars. As a matter of pitching instruction and inspiration, Indians coaches and instructors pointed to Kluber as the perfect possibility model, a man who had not merely mastered the daily preparatory routines of his craft with a robotic zen quality, but who had demonstrated how far that mastery can take a pitcher who, as a farmhand, had never been an idealized prospect. Broadly speaking, Bauer pursues an identical quest to be the best he can be, but his combination of conviction in and proselytization for his more tech-savvy process appears to have made him even more of a pain in the ass than just his picking fights on the internet.

Which is why what they do with Francisco Lindor is the defining choice for the organization. And this is where the legend of Sisyphus fails us as a metaphor, as grubby reality intrudes. Because like Sisyphus, the Indians are not stupid, and they reap the full measure of their ambition and actions. They haven't reached the top since that last World Series title in 1948. But it isn't like they're losing money, not when baseball is making more than $10 billion in a season while the

---

1. Yes, Joe Gordon and Birdie Tebbetts also achieved this in their multi-year stints, though without winning at least an AL pennant as Lopez and Francona did. Heck, even Ossie Vitt of "Cleveland Crybabies" infamy never had a losing season.

Indians' payroll might be found in the majors' bottom third. Money should not be a problem, not when there's more money sloshing around the industry than ever before.

The Indians are welcome to open their books and show us otherwise, of course. But until they do, it seems as if we can count on their ability to afford Lindor now, and afford the talent to put around him as well. Shedding the salaries of Kipnis and Kluber (not to mention Bauer) should buy Cleveland more than just Lindor's arbitration-fueled pay raise and second-base adequacy in the form of César Hernández. Much more. The Indians' ambitions embrace higher goals than adequacy on the cheap or cleverly buying back Carlos Santana on a fraction of his market price.

To make good on the two years left with Lindor, they will need more. The Twins and White Sox are threats, but beatable threats for the next two seasons. Pinching pennies during the final Lindor years the Indians have left to them would be a mistake; once he's gone, they won't be able to replace him. Once he scrams for 2022, the Indians could very well find themselves mired with the Royals and Tigers in Rust Belt ignominy and irrelevance.

That's in the uncertain future, a future that is beyond their control. The next two years, however, are theirs to win with. To try selling a Lindor deal to their fans, any time between now and his filing for free agency, instead of embracing the chance to actually get over their historic hump, would be as bleak a confession of "higher" priorities than winning within the industry as any that could be made. It would come at a time when tanking in the standings is tanking the entertainment value of multiple franchises. It's up to the Indians to rise above the temptation to accept they've won what they could with a Lindor-led roster, and embrace the privilege of employing him with all that entails—including spending to win.

—Christina Kahrl is a senior writer at ESPN.

Part 2: Player Analysis

PLAYER COMMENTS WITH GRAPHS

Greg Allen   OF

Born: 03/15/93   Age: 27   Bats: B   Throws: R
Height: 6'0"   Weight: 185   Origin: Round 6, 2014 Draft (#188 overall)

YEAR	TEAM	LVL	AGE	PA	R	2B	3B	HR	RBI	BB	K	SB	CS	AVG/OBP/SLG
2017	AKR	AA	24	303	37	16	1	2	24	22	55	21	2	.264/.344/.357
2017	CLE	MLB	24	39	7	1	0	1	6	2	8	1	0	.229/.282/.343
2018	COH	AAA	25	205	31	13	0	2	14	19	44	12	6	.298/.395/.409
2018	CLE	MLB	25	291	36	11	3	2	20	14	58	21	4	.257/.310/.343
2019	COH	AAA	26	226	37	9	3	5	17	20	44	10	5	.268/.358/.419
2019	CLE	MLB	26	256	30	9	3	4	27	11	53	8	2	.229/.290/.346
2020	CLE	MLB	27	280	27	13	1	5	27	18	57	12	4	.234/.307/.355

Comparables: Johnny Groth, Herm Winningham, Ruben Mateo

We've all had the pleasure of dining at the fine establishment known as McDonald's. It's fine. It's usually very fast. It's rarely offensive. Coincidentally, these adjectives can also sum up Allen's 2019 campaign, as the 26-year-old leaned on his speed to play passable outfield defense. The problem for Allen, however, was his production at the plate, where he hit like a decent pitcher as opposed to someone in the mix for everyday reps on a team with playoff aspirations. It's fair to assume that his existence as a starter might go the way of the Arch Deluxe, as opposed to the steady, reliability of the Big Mac.

YEAR	TEAM	LVL	AGE	PA	DRC+	VORP	BABIP	BRR	FRAA	WARP
2017	AKR	AA	24	303	93	12.7	.319	1.5	CF(67): -6.4, RF(1): -0.1	0.3
2017	CLE	MLB	24	39	75	0.6	.259	0.7	CF(21): -0.9, LF(5): -0.1	0.0
2018	COH	AAA	25	205	129	13.1	.389	0.3	CF(42): 2.3, LF(5): -0.4	1.5
2018	CLE	MLB	25	291	79	4.0	.320	3.4	CF(78): 2.8, RF(16): -0.4	0.8
2019	COH	AAA	26	226	95	9.5	.322	0.6	CF(25): 1.6, LF(15): 1.4	0.8
2019	CLE	MLB	26	256	74	-1.1	.280	0.8	LF(60): 6.0, CF(18): -1.6	0.4
2020	CLE	MLB	27	280	79	-0.1	.283	0.9	RF -3, CF 0	-0.2

Greg Allen, continued

Batted Ball Distribution

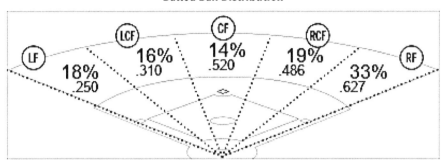

Strike Zone vs LHP   ### Strike Zone vs RHP

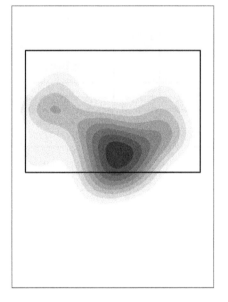

Jake Bauers   OF/1B

Born: 10/06/95   Age: 24   Bats: L   Throws: L
Height: 6'1"   Weight: 195   Origin: Round 7, 2013 Draft (#208 overall)

YEAR	TEAM	LVL	AGE	PA	R	2B	3B	HR	RBI	BB	K	SB	CS	AVG/OBP/SLG
2017	DUR	AAA	21	575	79	31	1	13	63	78	112	20	3	.263/.368/.412
2018	DUR	AAA	22	222	31	14	0	5	24	23	47	10	6	.279/.357/.426
2018	TBA	MLB	22	388	48	22	2	11	48	54	104	6	6	.201/.316/.384
2019	COH	AAA	23	103	13	7	0	3	15	14	26	8	2	.247/.350/.427
2019	CLE	MLB	23	423	46	16	1	12	43	45	115	3	3	.226/.312/.371
2020	CLE	MLB	24	455	49	19	1	15	52	50	120	7	3	.219/.310/.381

Comparables: Jon Singleton, Wayne Belardi, Freddie Freeman

The following takes place from March to September, 2019.

FADE IN: Our secret weapon, Jake Bauers (24), wipes sweat from his brow as he works tirelessly and deliberately to diffuse the bomb. Tick, tock. Tick, tock. He's speedy, to be sure, but has difficulty utilizing the power to effectively finish the task. He waits. And waits. And ultimately his patience, a calling card that separates him from other agents...uh, hitters, is used against him. The bomb explodes and he strikes out, leaving the debris of a 2019 season in its wake.

Boop Beep Boop Beep

YEAR	TEAM	LVL	AGE	PA	DRC+	VORP	BABIP	BRR	FRAA	WARP
2017	DUR	AAA	21	575	124	22.1	.314	0.5	LF(55): 4.7, 1B(52): -1.0	2.8
2018	DUR	AAA	22	222	128	12.0	.345	0.9	1B(46): -0.4, LF(4): 0.3	0.9
2018	TBA	MLB	22	388	86	8.2	.252	2.5	1B(76): -2.4, LF(16): 0.5	0.0
2019	COH	AAA	23	103	96	0.9	.317	0.1	LF(15): 2.1, 1B(6): 0.1	0.3
2019	CLE	MLB	23	423	85	0.5	.290	0.7	LF(53): 0.1, 1B(31): -2.2	-0.1
2020	CLE	MLB	24	455	84	2.7	.275	2.0	LF 4, 1B 0	0.6

Jake Bauers, continued

Batted Ball Distribution

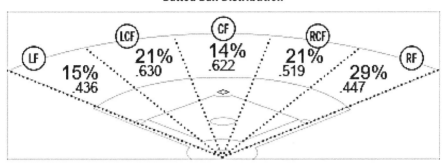

Strike Zone vs LHP   Strike Zone vs RHP

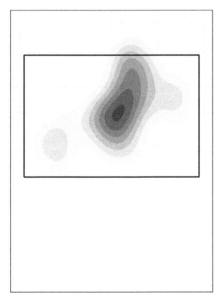 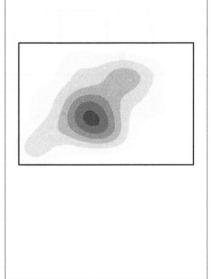

Yu Chang   INF

Born: 08/18/95   Age: 24   Bats: R   Throws: R
Height: 6'1"   Weight: 180   Origin: International Free Agent, 2013

YEAR	TEAM	LVL	AGE	PA	R	2B	3B	HR	RBI	BB	K	SB	CS	AVG/OBP/SLG
2017	AKR	AA	21	508	72	24	5	24	66	52	134	11	4	.220/.312/.461
2018	COH	AAA	22	518	56	28	2	13	62	44	144	4	3	.256/.330/.411
2019	COH	AAA	23	283	45	15	1	9	39	26	67	4	1	.253/.322/.427
2019	CLE	MLB	23	84	8	2	1	1	6	11	22	0	0	.178/.286/.274
2020	CLE	MLB	24	140	14	6	1	5	16	11	39	1	0	.205/.277/.371

Comparables: Gil McDougald, Jonathan Villar, Daniel Robertson

Chang debuted in 2019, making him just the fifth Taiwanese-born position player in big-league history. The results weren't great, as his strikeout problems followed him to the Show, but he displayed an aptitude for walking and playing defense on the left side of the infield. His ultimate landing spot (at least in Cleveland) will likely be at second base, which should help his chances for everyday reps.

YEAR	TEAM	LVL	AGE	PA	DRC+	VORP	BABIP	BRR	FRAA	WARP
2017	AKR	AA	21	508	102	33.9	.254	2.3	SS(122): 20.3	4.8
2018	COH	AAA	22	518	104	16.6	.341	-3.3	SS(94): -7.3, 3B(23): -0.7	1.1
2019	COH	AAA	23	283	93	8.2	.306	0.9	SS(22): 0.2, 2B(22): 0.4	0.8
2019	CLE	MLB	23	84	77	0.7	.240	-0.9	3B(25): -0.3, SS(8): -0.1	-0.1
2020	CLE	MLB	24	140	69	-1.4	.257	0.0	SS 1, 3B -1	-0.1

Yu Chang, continued

Batted Ball Distribution

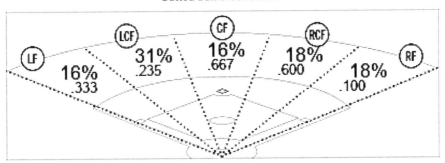

Strike Zone vs LHP   *Strike Zone vs RHP*

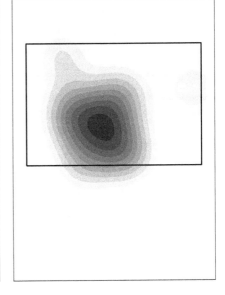

Delino DeShields CF

Born: 08/16/92   Age: 27   Bats: R   Throws: R
Height: 5'9"   Weight: 200   Origin: Round 1, 2010 Draft (#8 overall)

YEAR	TEAM	LVL	AGE	PA	R	2B	3B	HR	RBI	BB	K	SB	CS	AVG/OBP/SLG
2017	TEX	MLB	24	440	75	15	2	6	22	44	109	29	8	.269/.347/.367
2018	FRI	AA	25	26	2	0	0	0	0	8	2	2	2	.278/.500/.278
2018	TEX	MLB	25	393	52	14	1	2	22	43	83	20	4	.216/.310/.281
2019	NAS	AAA	26	75	10	3	0	3	11	8	17	8	0	.258/.338/.439
2019	TEX	MLB	26	408	42	15	4	4	32	38	100	24	6	.249/.325/.347
2020	CLE	MLB	27	280	27	11	1	4	24	28	69	14	4	.226/.311/.329

Comparables: Herm Winningham, Roy Sievers, Milton Bradley

It's coming to the point in DeShields' career that he's going to have to take the Ferrell/Carrey split. Both actors were known early in their career for doing one thing really well. Ferrell yelled at the camera in nearly the same voice as a step-brother, a racecar driver, an anchorman and numerous other roles. Carrey was the rubber-faced over-actor, gesturing wildly as he contorted his face into impossibly emotive shapes. As each actor hit the saturation point, they had to make a decision. Carrey adjusted, carrying such chops-forward films as Truman Show, 23 and the heavy-but-quirky Eternal Sunshine of the Spotless Mind. Ferrell did try that one weird Spanish movie, but largely just kept yelling in the same way he always had. How does this have anything to do with Delino DeShields? He's been a speedster his entire life. It's the first thing anyone says about him: he's fast. So far, that's been enough to make up for any other deficiencies in his game. But now he's entering his late 20s, meaning his legs will start to let him down within the next few years. If he can keep adding improvements—as he did with his defense a couple of years ago—he'll be able to retire on his own terms and get as weird as he wants. If not, the turn of the decade might be less "Good Guys" and more "Holmes and Watson."

YEAR	TEAM	LVL	AGE	PA	DRC+	VORP	BABIP	BRR	FRAA	WARP
2017	TEX	MLB	24	440	86	13.8	.358	7.6	LF(60): 4.3, CF(51): -0.5	1.7
2018	FRI	AA	25	26	176	0.6	.313	-0.9	CF(5): -0.5	0.1
2018	TEX	MLB	25	393	73	1.0	.280	3.4	CF(102): 10.3	1.5
2019	NAS	AAA	26	75	93	5.8	.304	1.6	CF(13): 1.1, LF(1): 0.8	0.5
2019	TEX	MLB	26	408	77	2.9	.333	4.9	CF(112): 6.9	1.4
2020	CLE	MLB	27	280	75	3.5	.296	2.4	CF 4	0.8

Delino DeShields, continued

Batted Ball Distribution

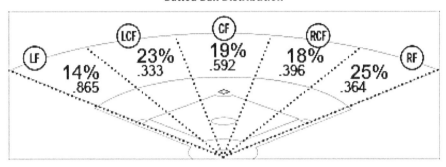

Strike Zone vs LHP

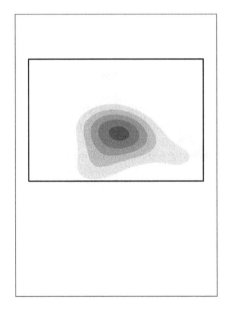

Strike Zone vs RHP

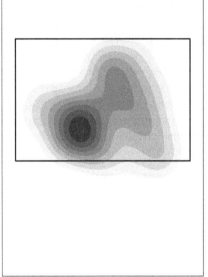

Mike Freeman   UT

Born: 08/04/87   Age: 32   Bats: L   Throws: R
Height: 6'0"   Weight: 195   Origin: Round 11, 2010 Draft (#331 overall)

YEAR	TEAM	LVL	AGE	PA	R	2B	3B	HR	RBI	BB	K	SB	CS	AVG/OBP/SLG
2017	TAC	AAA	29	67	12	3	1	1	9	7	10	2	0	.350/.418/.483
2017	OKL	AAA	29	139	17	4	2	0	16	13	31	5	0	.306/.384/.372
2017	IOW	AAA	29	88	10	3	0	2	6	7	19	3	0	.273/.345/.390
2017	SEA	MLB	29	34	3	0	0	1	1	4	9	0	0	.067/.176/.167
2017	LAN	MLB	29	5	0	0	0	0	0	0	2	0	0	.000/.000/.000
2017	CHN	MLB	29	27	3	2	0	0	0	2	8	0	0	.160/.222/.240
2018	IOW	AAA	30	331	51	15	2	6	38	25	66	6	6	.274/.330/.396
2018	CHN	MLB	30	1	0	0	0	0	0	0	0	0	0	
2019	COH	AAA	31	33	6	0	0	3	3	9	7	1	0	.208/.424/.583
2019	CLE	MLB	31	213	27	8	0	4	24	22	61	1	2	.277/.362/.390
2020	CLE	MLB	32	35	3	1	0	1	3	3	10	0	0	.218/.295/.318

Comparables: Collin Cowgill, Ferris Fain, Alex Presley

Freeman strode to the plate more times last season than the rest of his big-league career *combined*, and would you believe he looked the part of a useful utility player? Heck, he was even called upon for mop-up duty during a 13-0 drubbing against the Orioles. Freeman was an intimidating presence on the bump, ranging from 64-76 mph with his "fastball" and breaking off a curveball that certainly had the intent of being a curveball. He immediately induced a groundout, but ran into some turbulence that ruined his perfect ERA. He did cruise to another scoreless inning afterward, though, and should get a chance to replicate what he actually gets paid to do—hitting, but mostly being able to defend multiple positions—in 2020.

YEAR	TEAM	LVL	AGE	PA	DRC+	VORP	BABIP	BRR	FRAA	WARP
2017	TAC	AAA	29	67	99	6.9	.408	0.7	2B(9): 0.5, 3B(6): -0.1	0.4
2017	OKL	AAA	29	139	100	5.6	.407	1.5	SS(14): 1.7, 3B(14): -0.1	0.8
2017	IOW	AAA	29	88	101	4.0	.333	-0.6	SS(11): -0.1, 3B(7): -1.3	0.2
2017	SEA	MLB	29	34	57	-3.4	.050	0.2	2B(3): -0.2, 1B(3): 0.3	-0.1
2017	LAN	MLB	29	5	57	-1.3	.000	0.0	3B(1): 0.0	0.0
2017	CHN	MLB	29	27	58	-1.7	.235	-0.1	SS(10): 0.0, 2B(3): 0.0	0.0
2018	IOW	AAA	30	331	101	21.2	.332	1.8	SS(55): 2.7, 2B(16): -0.1	1.9
2018	CHN	MLB	30	1	91	0.0	--	0.0	2B(1): 0.0	0.0
2019	COH	AAA	31	33	147	2.6	.143	0.0	SS(4): 0.2, 3B(2): 0.2	0.3
2019	CLE	MLB	31	213	78	1.7	.388	1.3	2B(33): 2.1, 3B(18): -0.1	0.4
2020	CLE	MLB	32	35	66	0.0	.297	0.1	2B 0	0.0

Mike Freeman, continued

Batted Ball Distribution

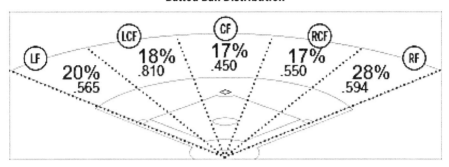

Strike Zone vs LHP   ## Strike Zone vs RHP

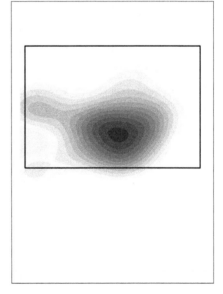

César Hernández 2B

Born: 05/23/90   Age: 30   Bats: B   Throws: R
Height: 5'10"   Weight: 160   Origin: International Free Agent, 2006

YEAR	TEAM	LVL	AGE	PA	R	2B	3B	HR	RBI	BB	K	SB	CS	AVG/OBP/SLG
2017	PHI	MLB	27	577	85	26	6	9	34	61	104	15	5	.294/.373/.421
2018	PHI	MLB	28	708	91	15	3	15	60	95	155	19	6	.253/.356/.362
2019	PHI	MLB	29	667	77	31	3	14	71	45	100	9	2	.279/.333/.408
2020	CLE	MLB	30	560	57	23	3	11	56	49	100	14	6	.264/.333/.384

Comparables: Jerome Walton, Herm Winningham, Dave Martinez

For the last few years, Hernández has been profiled in this space as a good player who was underrated and misunderstood by the talk-radio airheads on both sides of the telephone. Score one for the airheads last year, as Hernandez slipped significantly on both sides of the ball. Hernández took a far more free-swinging approach than ever, and while the strikeouts didn't increase, he lost more with the lack of walks than he gained with additional weakly batted balls in play. The mental miscues that have always been part of the package with Hernández are easier to overlook when he's having a three-WARP campaign than when he's hovering barely over replacement level. Even on a team of players who generally underperformed, Hernández's slippage stood out. He'll try to regroup in Cleveland.

YEAR	TEAM	LVL	AGE	PA	DRC+	VORP	BABIP	BRR	FRAA	WARP
2017	PHI	MLB	27	577	103	35.8	.353	4.2	2B(127): -2.4, SS(1): 0.0	2.2
2018	PHI	MLB	28	708	101	30.7	.315	2.0	2B(154): 3.7	2.9
2019	PHI	MLB	29	667	90	13.7	.313	-1.2	2B(157): -4.7	0.8
2020	CLE	MLB	30	560	94	19.2	.312	0.7	2B -1	1.9

César Hernández, continued

Batted Ball Distribution

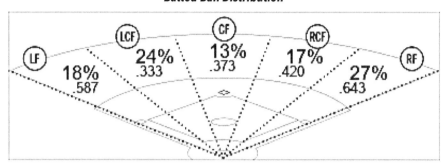

Strike Zone vs LHP **Strike Zone vs RHP**

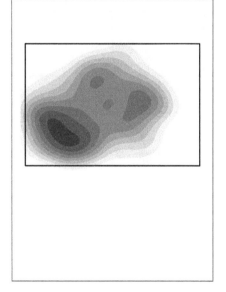

Sandy León C

Born: 03/13/89   Age: 31   Bats: B   Throws: R
Height: 5'10"   Weight: 225   Origin: International Free Agent, 2007

YEAR	TEAM	LVL	AGE	PA	R	2B	3B	HR	RBI	BB	K	SB	CS	AVG/OBP/SLG
2017	BOS	MLB	28	301	32	14	0	7	39	25	74	0	0	.225/.290/.354
2018	BOS	MLB	29	288	30	12	0	5	22	15	75	1	0	.177/.232/.279
2019	BOS	MLB	30	191	14	3	0	5	19	13	47	0	0	.192/.251/.297
2020	CLE	MLD	31	245	22	9	0	6	24	18	63	1	0	.210/.275/.334

Comparables: Miguel Montero, Brandon Inge, Randy Knorr

Any marketer knows that brand loyalty is among the most difficult concepts to measure, maintain and instill in a consumer base. Perhaps they should all consult León, who continued to convince the Red Sox to use his services despite the many superior

YEAR	TEAM	P. COUNT	FRM RUNS	BLK RUNS	THRW RUNS	TOT RUNS
2017	BOS	11373	9.7	0.4	2.0	10.7
2018	BOS	11107	11.6	0.1	0.1	11.7
2019	BOS	8115	4.8	-1.0	-0.2	3.5
2020	CLE	11942	2.0	-0.3	0.5	2.2

options on the market. Defense has long been León's *raison d'etre*, but he is declining as a receiver, framer and thrower at this point. Offensively, well, the most polite thing we can say is that León hasn't posted a DRC+ north of 100 since 2016. (If one wished to be impolite, one could point out that the remains of Carlos González, Mark Reynolds and *literally Gordon Beckham* all provided more value as hitters in 2019.) Even León's familiarity with the underperforming Boston pitching staff didn't carry enough weight to keep him around in the end, but he'll function as a better backup in Cleveland than Kevin Plawecki.

YEAR	TEAM	LVL	AGE	PA	DRC+	VORP	BABIP	BRR	FRAA	WARP
2017	BOS	MLB	28	301	74	-2.0	.280	-5.2	C(84): 10.8	1.1
2018	BOS	MLB	29	288	58	-1.4	.226	-0.7	C(87): 11.7	1.1
2019	BOS	MLB	30	191	65	1.4	.231	-0.2	C(65): 2.9, 1B(1): 0.0	0.4
2020	CLE	MLB	31	245	63	-1.8	.265	-1.4	C 1	-0.1

Sandy León, continued

Batted Ball Distribution

Strike Zone vs LHP   *Strike Zone vs RHP*

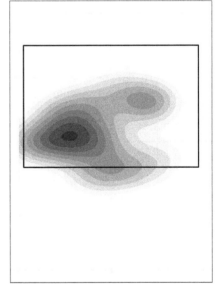

Francisco Lindor SS

Born: 11/14/93   Age: 26   Bats: B   Throws: R
Height: 5'11"   Weight: 190   Origin: Round 1, 2011 Draft (#8 overall)

YEAR	TEAM	LVL	AGE	PA	R	2B	3B	HR	RBI	BB	K	SB	CS	AVG/OBP/SLG
2017	CLE	MLB	23	723	99	44	4	33	89	60	93	15	3	.273/.337/.505
2018	CLE	MLB	24	745	129	42	2	38	92	70	107	25	10	.277/.352/.519
2019	CLE	MLB	25	654	101	40	2	32	74	46	98	22	5	.284/.335/.518
2020	CLE	MLB	26	630	80	35	2	30	92	49	96	15	5	.273/.333/.495

Comparables: Ketel Marte, Orlando Arcia, Jorge Polanco

Let's talk smiles. Mona Lisa's? Classic. Sly, yet alluring. She knows something, but she's not telling. Jack Nicholson? No wait, the Joker—eh, no, let's just do regular Jack, because then we get "The Shining" Jack and "A Few Good Men" Jack. It's mischievous, but somehow also warm and exciting. What about Magic Johnson? Excellence and confidence. Julia Roberts, more specifically, Julia in "Pretty Woman"—it was an announcement, an arrival. How good of a smile do you have to have in order to wear "Mr. Smile" on your back for Players' Weekend? As it turns out, a pretty good one.

Lindor's smile is the absolute perfect encapsulation of him as a player. His smile is sheer joy and authority. It's pure. Lots of young stars start their careers this way, sure, but somehow Lindor has managed to maintain that exuberance on his ascent to superstardom. Despite missing roughly the first month of the campaign, he still smacked 30 homers and snagged 15 bags for the third consecutive season.

During the extension-happy portion offseason, Cleveland's owner Paul Dolan was asked about signing Lindor for the long term. Dolan's response: "Enjoy him." It was unnecessary, frustrating and ominous. Smiles don't last, but turning a smile into a frown is dastardly. It was, in a sense, the exact opposite of why people love Lindor and the game—and the reason why smiles seem to be harder to come by in baseball, be it on the field or in the stands, where happy faces have been replaced by empty seatbacks.

YEAR	TEAM	LVL	AGE	PA	DRC+	VORP	BABIP	BRR	FRAA	WARP
2017	CLE	MLB	23	723	118	49.8	.275	2.1	SS(158): 3.8	5.5
2018	CLE	MLB	24	745	128	57.9	.279	-0.5	SS(157): 5.9	6.5
2019	CLE	MLB	25	654	117	45.7	.291	-2.3	SS(137): -4.8	3.8
2020	CLE	MLB	26	630	117	36.0	.282	-0.6	SS 1	3.8

Francisco Lindor, continued

Batted Ball Distribution

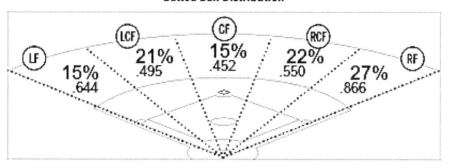

Strike Zone vs LHP

Strike Zone vs RHP

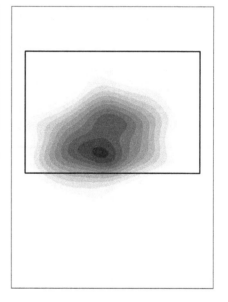

Jordan Luplow OF

Born: 09/26/93   Age: 26   Bats: R   Throws: R
Height: 6'1"   Weight: 195   Origin: Round 3, 2014 Draft (#100 overall)

YEAR	TEAM	LVL	AGE	PA	R	2B	3B	HR	RBI	BB	K	SB	CS	AVG/OBP/SLG
2017	ALT	AA	23	288	45	15	0	16	37	29	45	1	3	.287/.368/.535
2017	IND	AAA	23	182	29	7	1	7	19	16	36	4	1	.325/.401/.513
2017	PIT	MLB	23	87	6	3	1	3	11	6	22	0	1	.205/.276/.385
2018	IND	AAA	24	357	41	25	3	8	49	39	64	7	2	.287/.367/.462
2018	PIT	MLB	24	103	16	1	3	3	7	10	18	2	2	.185/.272/.359
2019	COH	AAA	25	57	12	3	0	2	7	10	14	2	1	.311/.456/.511
2019	CLE	MLB	25	261	42	15	1	15	38	33	61	3	2	.276/.372/.551
2020	CLE	MLB	26	175	23	8	1	9	26	18	41	1	1	.240/.328/.472

Comparables: Mike Young, Jeff Burroughs, Matt Joyce

When Cleveland acquired Luplow, a reasonable goal was to strengthen their lineup against left-handers by being better than Brandon Guyer. He checked off both boxes by hitting southpaws to the tune of a .320/.439/.742 slash line in 128 trips to the plate. Unfortunately, thanks to a dearth of big-league quality outfielders in Cleveland this season, he also played against righties. That didn't go as well. Still, he finished as a well-above-average hitter overall and looks like a savvy pickup and useful player.

YEAR	TEAM	LVL	AGE	PA	DRC+	VORP	BABIP	BRR	FRAA	WARP
2017	ALT	AA	23	288	149	25.9	.294	1.5	LF(65): 4.3, 3B(1): 0.0	2.8
2017	IND	AAA	23	182	163	18.0	.381	-0.8	LF(27): 3.4, RF(15): 0.9	1.9
2017	PIT	MLB	23	87	77	-1.4	.241	-0.4	RF(14): 0.1, LF(10): 0.7	0.0
2018	IND	AAA	24	357	146	20.4	.336	-1.7	LF(41): 4.3, RF(38): 1.4	2.8
2018	PIT	MLB	24	103	85	-2.7	.197	-0.4	LF(16): 5.4, RF(11): -0.3	0.6
2019	COH	AAA	25	57	126	3.3	.414	-0.5	LF(10): 1.5, RF(2): -0.2	0.4
2019	CLE	MLB	25	261	126	15.5	.313	0.3	RF(42): 3.4, LF(34): 0.3	1.9
2020	CLE	MLB	26	175	107	5.8	.269	0.2	RF-1, LF 2	0.7

Jordan Luplow, continued

Batted Ball Distribution

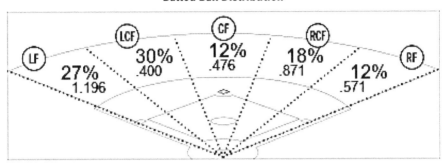

Strike Zone vs LHP

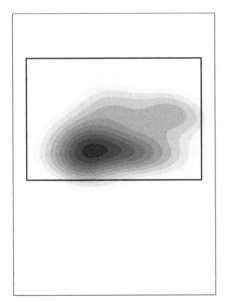

Strike Zone vs RHP

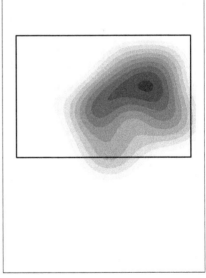

Oscar Mercado CF

Born: 12/16/94   Age: 25   Bats: R   Throws: R
Height: 6'2"   Weight: 197   Origin: Round 2, 2013 Draft (#57 overall)

YEAR	TEAM	LVL	AGE	PA	R	2B	3B	HR	RBI	BB	K	SB	CS	AVG/OBP/SLG
2017	SFD	AA	22	523	76	20	4	13	46	32	112	38	19	.287/.341/.428
2018	MEM	AAA	23	427	73	21	1	8	42	36	64	31	8	.285/.351/.408
2018	COH	AAA	23	119	12	5	1	0	5	13	23	6	4	.252/.342/.320
2019	COH	AAA	24	140	24	10	1	4	15	16	32	14	3	.294/.396/.496
2019	CLE	MLB	24	482	70	25	3	15	54	28	84	15	4	.269/.318/.443
2020	CLE	MLB	25	560	59	28	2	15	61	37	111	29	13	.241/.301/.389

Comparables: Roy Sievers, Rip Repulski, Rondell White

In a sense, Mercado had a typical rookie season, complete with stretches of brilliance (usually on defense) and bouts of frustration. Oddly, his trademark patience didn't make the trip to the big leagues. He did maintain an above-average contact rate that helped him eschew strikeouts and showcase his plus speed. Although never known for his power, he took full advantage of the rabbit ball to hit 15 home runs. Mercado looks a bit like the Ender Inciarte starter kit, and that should be enough for him to remain a starting center fielder.

YEAR	TEAM	LVL	AGE	PA	DRC+	VORP	BABIP	BRR	FRAA	WARP
2017	SFD	AA	22	523	114	35.1	.348	5.7	CF(108): -2.1, LF(7): -0.7	2.7
2018	MEM	AAA	23	427	108	32.6	.323	8.1	CF(89): -2.6, LF(7): -0.5	2.4
2018	COH	AAA	23	119	93	-2.3	.325	-2.2	CF(24): -0.8, RF(7): 0.3	0.0
2019	COH	AAA	24	140	129	11.6	.373	1.1	CF(19): 5.4, LF(5): 1.1	1.5
2019	CLE	MLB	24	482	97	15.0	.300	2.3	CF(82): 8.3, LF(24): -1.6	2.2
2020	CLE	MLB	25	560	81	3.5	.281	0.3	CF 2, LF -1	0.4

Oscar Mercado, continued

Batted Ball Distribution

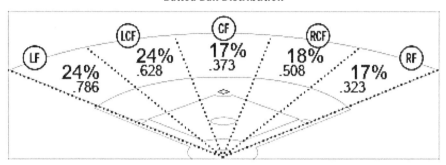

LF **24%** .786   LCF **24%** .628   CF **17%** .373   RCF **18%** .508   **17%** .323 RF

Strike Zone vs LHP   Strike Zone vs RHP

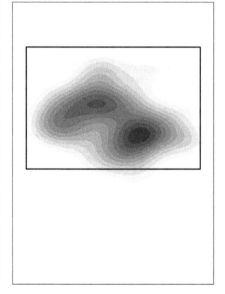

Tyler Naquin   RF

Born: 04/24/91   Age: 29   Bats: L   Throws: R
Height: 6'2"   Weight: 195   Origin: Round 1, 2012 Draft (#15 overall)

YEAR	TEAM	LVL	AGE	PA	R	2B	3B	HR	RBI	BB	K	SB	CS	AVG/OBP/SLG
2017	COH	AAA	26	330	42	14	4	10	51	30	71	5	2	.298/.359/.475
2017	CLE	MLB	26	40	4	2	0	0	1	2	9	0	1	.216/.250/.270
2018	CLE	MLB	27	183	22	7	0	3	23	6	42	1	1	.264/.295/.356
2019	CLE	MLB	28	294	34	19	0	10	34	14	66	4	2	.288/.325/.467
2020	CLE	MLB	29	280	31	15	1	10	35	19	72	4	2	.261/.318/.438

Comparables: Abraham Almonte, Lorenzo Cain, Roger Bernadina

Dinner rolls are good; sometimes they're even great. You just don't want to have an entire meal comprised of dinner rolls. It's kind of like Naquin's involvement in the Cleveland outfield. He's fine to have around, but he's at his best when he's the third or fourth most important part of the experience. A team can get into trouble if they need him to provide more than that. A shift to a corner-outfield spot has helped Naquin defensively, as he led all outfielders in FRAA. That value helps offset his bat—he's now been a below-average hitter for three consecutive seasons. He's best when warm and dipped in gravy.

YEAR	TEAM	LVL	AGE	PA	DRC+	VORP	BABIP	BRR	FRAA	WARP
2017	COH	AAA	26	330	122	18.3	.358	0.9	CF(49): 10.7, RF(23): -1.1	2.6
2017	CLE	MLB	26	40	73	-1.4	.276	-0.2	CF(11): -0.4, RF(8): -0.5	-0.1
2018	CLE	MLB	27	183	79	1.3	.331	1.0	RF(39): 5.2, CF(19): 0.2	0.6
2019	CLE	MLB	28	294	93	4.6	.345	-0.3	RF(68): 12.2, LF(15): 4.1	2.0
2020	CLE	MLB	29	280	98	6.3	.327	0.3	LF 5, RF 5	1.6

Tyler Naquin, continued

Batted Ball Distribution

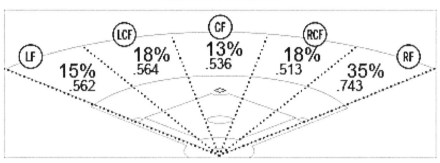

Strike Zone vs LHP   ## Strike Zone vs RHP

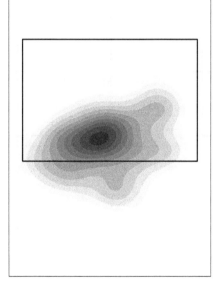

Yasiel Puig   RF

Born: 12/07/90   Age: 29   Bats: R   Throws: R
Height: 6'2"   Weight: 240   Origin: International Free Agent, 2012

YEAR	TEAM	LVL	AGE	PA	R	2B	3B	HR	RBI	BB	K	SB	CS	AVG/OBP/SLG
2017	LAN	MLB	26	570	72	24	2	28	74	64	100	15	6	.263/.346/.487
2018	LAN	MLB	27	444	60	21	1	23	63	36	87	15	5	.267/.327/.494
2019	CLE	MLB	28	207	25	15	1	2	23	21	44	5	2	.297/.377/.423
2019	CIN	MLB	28	404	51	15	1	22	61	23	89	14	5	.252/.302/.475
2020	CLE	MLB	29	575	70	27	2	24	77	48	130	12	5	.260/.330/.457

Comparables: Travis Buck, Justin Upton, Jay Bruce

Just when you think you've seen everything Puig has to offer—an exciting play, a humorous celebration, a bewildering gaffe—he goes and delivers something like his Cleveland stint. Puig homered 24 times in 2019, the second-most of his career. Yet 22 of those came with the Reds; in 49 games with Cleveland, he cleared the fences twice, and instead prioritized hitting for average and getting on base. It was an odd, presumably intentional shift for someone heading to free agency—and one that, frankly, leaves us wondering what's coming next. That Puig, he's baseball's best at keeping us engaged.

YEAR	TEAM	LVL	AGE	PA	DRC+	VORP	BABIP	BRR	FRAA	WARP
2017	LAN	MLB	26	570	119	27.1	.274	-4.3	RF(145): 9.0	3.1
2018	LAN	MLB	27	444	120	23.7	.286	2.4	RF(118): -4.5	1.9
2019	CLE	MLB	28	207	101	5.3	.380	-1.5	RF(48): 2.7	0.6
2019	CIN	MLB	28	404	101	10.1	.272	-2.8	RF(98): 2.1	0.9
2020	CLE	MLB	29	575	106	9.3	.305	-2.3	RF 0	2.2

Yasiel Puig, continued

Batted Ball Distribution

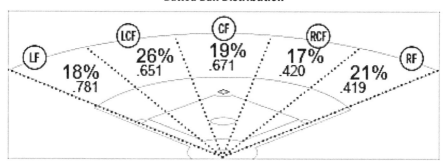

Strike Zone vs LHP   ## Strike Zone vs RHP

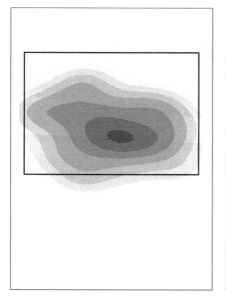   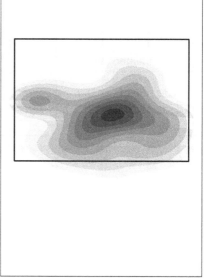

Roberto Pérez   C

Born: 12/23/88   Age: 31   Bats: R   Throws: R
Height: 5'11"   Weight: 220   Origin: Round 33, 2008 Draft (#1011 overall)

YEAR	TEAM	LVL	AGE	PA	R	2B	3B	HR	RBI	BB	K	SB	CS	AVG/OBP/SLG
2017	CLE	MLB	28	248	22	12	0	8	38	26	71	0	1	.207/.291/.373
2018	CLE	MLB	29	210	16	9	1	2	19	21	70	1	0	.168/.256/.263
2019	CLE	MLB	30	449	46	9	1	24	63	45	127	0	0	.239/.321/.452
2020	CLE	MLB	31	420	47	15	1	16	51	46	122	1	1	.212/.303/.390

Comparables: Sal Fasano, Alex Avila, Chris Herrmann

If Francisco Lindor is the face of the Indians, Pérez might be the heart. The long-time backup backstop finally got a chance for regular reps last season, and emerged as a no-doubt starter. Pérez notched 449 trips to the plate, over 200 more than any previous

YEAR	TEAM	P. COUNT	FRM RUNS	BLK RUNS	THRW RUNS	TOT RUNS
2017	CLE	9658	17.6	2.2	0.4	19.7
2018	CLE	7861	10.9	1.6	-0.2	12.1
2019	CLE	16272	15.5	8.8	1.5	25.6
2020	CLE	18552	18.2	4.6	2.5	25.2

season of his career, and more than doubled his career home-run total in the process. On the other side of the plate, Pérez was the second-best defender in baseball, per FRAA, behind only Austin Hedges. He led the league in blocking runs, and finished in the top three for runs saved via framing and throwing. Pérez, who signed a four-year, $9 million extension with two club options in 2017, was one of the 25 most valuable position players in baseball according to WARP. That's not an outcome anyone saw coming, but it's a welcomed one all the same.

YEAR	TEAM	LVL	AGE	PA	DRC+	VORP	BABIP	BRR	FRAA	WARP
2017	CLE	MLB	28	248	80	4.0	.266	-0.6	C(71): 19.8	2.5
2018	CLE	MLB	29	210	52	-4.5	.257	-0.2	C(58): 11.1	0.9
2019	CLE	MLB	30	449	100	24.0	.285	-1.1	C(118): 25.7	4.7
2020	CLE	MLB	31	420	82	9.2	.268	-0.6	C 25	3.5

Roberto Pérez, continued

Batted Ball Distribution

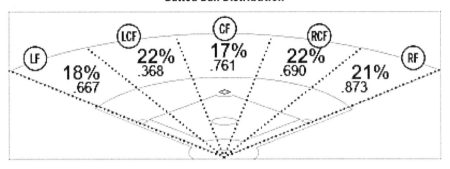

Strike Zone vs LHP

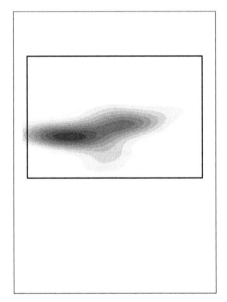

Strike Zone vs RHP

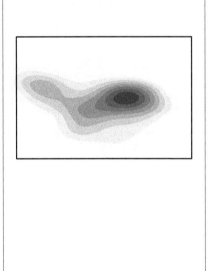

José Ramírez   3B

Born: 09/17/92   Age: 27   Bats: B   Throws: R
Height: 5'9"   Weight: 190   Origin: International Free Agent, 2009

YEAR	TEAM	LVL	AGE	PA	R	2B	3B	HR	RBI	BB	K	SB	CS	AVG/OBP/SLG
2017	CLE	MLB	24	645	107	56	6	29	83	52	69	17	5	.318/.374/.583
2018	CLE	MLB	25	698	110	38	4	39	105	106	80	34	6	.270/.387/.552
2019	CLE	MLB	26	542	68	33	3	23	83	52	74	24	4	.255/.327/.479
2020	CLE	MLB	27	560	71	33	2	25	79	54	75	18	5	.259/.334/.482

Comparables: Zoilo Versalles, Francisco Lindor, Wilmer Flores

There's an urban legend contained within Cleveland's fan base that Ramírez, world-renowned Mario Kart stud, went into a tailspin after suffering a shocking defeat at the hands of Shane Bieber. If that's true—and Lord knows it's probably not—he wasn't over the loss by the start of the 2019 campaign, as the former-All Star limped to a .212/.323/.349 line from August 1, 2018 to July 1, 2019. Yet Ramírez must've had a blue shell handy, because from that point forward he resumed pulling the ball and producing like an elite hitter—he slashed .321/.356/.722, and even returned late in the season from a broken hamate bone to homer twice in his first game back. We're not buying into the idea that Ramírez's play is connected with his pay ... but, just to be safe, Cleveland should institute a Yoshi court fine for anyone who makes an earnest attempt to defeat Ramírez.

YEAR	TEAM	LVL	AGE	PA	DRC+	VORP	BABIP	BRR	FRAA	WARP
2017	CLE	MLB	24	645	137	58.5	.319	0.2	3B(88): 6.0, 2B(71): -0.1	5.8
2018	CLE	MLB	25	698	146	69.9	.252	5.2	3B(137): -3.5, 2B(16): -0.7	6.6
2019	CLE	MLB	26	542	115	31.8	.256	2.6	3B(126): 2.4	3.6
2020	CLE	MLB	27	560	113	24.4	.261	1.0	3B -2	2.3

José Ramírez, continued

Batted Ball Distribution

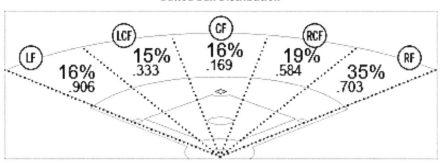

Strike Zone vs LHP

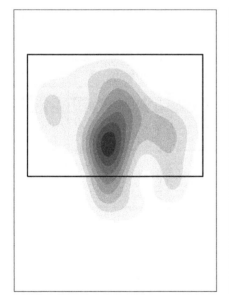

Strike Zone vs RHP

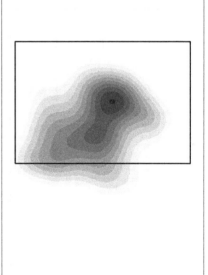

Franmil Reyes DH

Born: 07/07/95   Age: 24   Bats: R   Throws: R
Height: 6'5"   Weight: 275   Origin: International Free Agent, 2012

YEAR	TEAM	LVL	AGE	PA	R	2B	3B	HR	RBI	BB	K	SB	CS	AVG/OBP/SLG
2017	SAN	AA	21	566	79	27	1	25	102	48	134	4	4	.258/.322/.464
2018	ELP	AAA	22	250	50	11	1	16	52	37	59	0	0	.324/.428/.614
2018	SDN	MLB	22	285	36	9	0	16	31	24	80	0	0	.280/.340/.498
2019	SDN	MLB	23	354	43	9	0	27	46	29	93	0	0	.255/.314/.536
2019	CLE	MLB	23	194	26	10	0	10	35	18	63	0	0	.237/.304/.468
2020	CLE	MLB	24	525	73	24	1	34	89	45	147	1	1	.258/.323/.527

Comparables: Yorman Rodriguez, Randal Grichuk, Ronald Guzmán

It took Reyes 11 games to launch his first dinger after being shipped from San Diego to Cleveland. From that point on, he homered around once every three games, flirting with a .900 OPS down the stretch. Despite spreading out 37 home runs over two leagues, Reyes's huge power numbers didn't come with a side of sunshine and rainbows. Of 140 qualified hitters, nobody made less contact than he did, and only Javier Báez swung and missed more frequently. It's an issue that Reyes will need to address if he's ever going to make the leap to stardom. On the bright side, his hop to the AL will likely correspond with entry into the hallowed Full-Time DH Club, which is a positive for humanity.

YEAR	TEAM	LVL	AGE	PA	DRC+	VORP	BABIP	BRR	FRAA	WARP
2017	SAN	AA	21	566	120	27.8	.298	-1.1	RF(89): 3.2	2.3
2018	ELP	AAA	22	250	162	20.3	.382	1.9	RF(46): -2.2	2.3
2018	SDN	MLB	22	285	112	14.8	.345	0.3	RF(75): -7.1	0.3
2019	SDN	MLB	23	354	114	15.0	.268	0.4	RF(83): 1.4	1.6
2019	CLE	MLB	23	194	106	4.7	.301	-0.8	RF(3): 0.6	0.4
2020	CLE	MLB	24	525	115	16.4	.299	-0.1	RF 0	1.7

Franmil Reyes, continued

Batted Ball Distribution

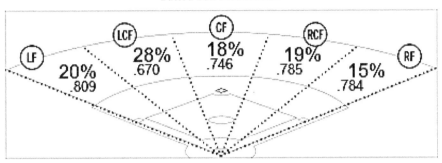

Strike Zone vs LHP   **Strike Zone vs RHP**

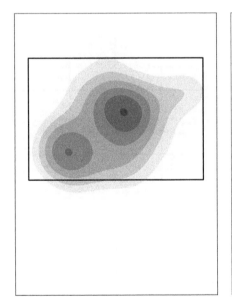   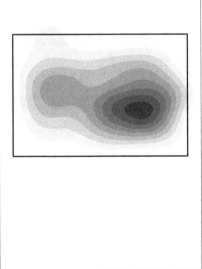

Carlos Santana   1B

Born: 04/08/86   Age: 34   Bats: B   Throws: R
Height: 5'11"   Weight: 210   Origin: International Free Agent, 2004

YEAR	TEAM	LVL	AGE	PA	R	2B	3B	HR	RBI	BB	K	SB	CS	AVG/OBP/SLG
2017	CLE	MLB	31	667	90	37	3	23	79	88	94	5	1	.259/.363/.455
2018	PHI	MLB	32	679	82	28	2	24	86	110	93	2	1	.229/.352/.414
2019	CLE	MLB	33	686	110	30	1	34	93	108	108	4	0	.281/.397/.515
2020	CLE	MLB	34	595	80	28	1	26	82	94	104	5	2	.256/.376/.470

Comparables: Chris Iannetta, Duke Sims, Mike Napoli

Santana's one-year sabbatical in Philly was a typical Santana season. He smacked 24 homers, walked a ton and played solid defense at the cold corner. One distinguishing scene, however, was Santana destroying a television after seeing teammates playing Fortnite during the final series of the year. We know that virtual reality is the next big thing in training, but that entails swinging in front of a screen to improve—not swinging *at* it. Nonetheless, the act of destruction transferred new electricity to Santana's bat, and in 2019 he enjoyed the best offensive season of his career. He came out of the gates hot, slashing .297/.418/.540 before the break, permitting him his first All-Star Game appearance and the honor of starting in his home ballpark. Our guess is that Santana will fall back in line with his usual output: a good on-base percentage, 20-plus homers and zero destroyed televisions.

YEAR	TEAM	LVL	AGE	PA	DRC+	VORP	BABIP	BRR	FRAA	WARP
2017	CLE	MLB	31	667	114	18.7	.274	-1.9	1B(140): 6.2, RF(7): 0.7	2.6
2018	PHI	MLB	32	679	108	26.1	.231	0.2	1B(149): -0.7, 3B(19): 0.6	1.8
2019	CLE	MLB	33	686	138	44.3	.293	1.1	1B(135): 3.9	4.8
2020	CLE	MLB	34	595	125	30.4	.276	-0.4	1B 1	3.3

Carlos Santana, continued

Batted Ball Distribution

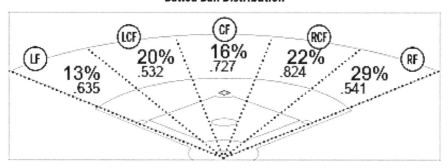

Strike Zone vs LHP   Strike Zone vs RHP

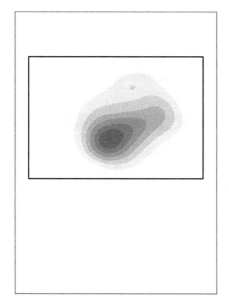 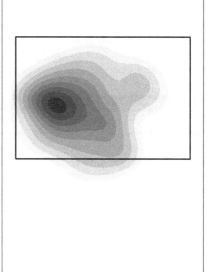

Domingo Santana   OF

Born: 08/05/92   Age: 27   Bats: R   Throws: R
Height: 6'5"   Weight: 220   Origin: International Free Agent, 2009

YEAR	TEAM	LVL	AGE	PA	R	2B	3B	HR	RBI	BB	K	SB	CS	AVG/OBP/SLG
2017	MIL	MLB	24	607	88	29	0	30	85	73	178	15	4	.278/.371/.505
2018	CSP	AAA	25	227	30	10	2	8	35	36	75	2	0	.283/.401/.487
2018	MIL	MLB	25	235	21	14	1	5	20	20	77	1	1	.265/.328/.412
2019	SEA	MLB	26	507	63	20	1	21	69	50	164	8	3	.253/.329/.441
2020	SEA	MLB	27	251	31	11	0	10	33	28	81	3	1	.248/.336/.442

Comparables: Carlos Delgado, Pete Incaviglia, Melvin Nieves

The first of 154 regular-season grand slams, second-most in history, was hit at roughly 3:30 AM Seattle time, when Santana flicked an opposite-field fly over the 329-foot marker against the A's in the Tokyo Dome on March 20. He went on to contribute 20 more long balls to the cause, 17 of which came before the All-Star Break. A hot first half suggested that playing time was in fact all Santana needed to prove himself as a legitimate offensive weapon, recapturing the form he flashed in Milwaukee in 2017. Unfortunately, a mid-season elbow injury shelved the hulking outfielder for several weeks and continued to hamper him once he returned to action down the stretch. Once a promising young prospect himself, Santana found himself a victim of baseball's new fad of non-tendering players who might be eligible for raises in arbitration.

YEAR	TEAM	LVL	AGE	PA	DRC+	VORP	BABIP	BRR	FRAA	WARP
2017	MIL	MLB	24	607	118	39.6	.363	0.2	RF(144): -7.7	2.0
2018	CSP	AAA	25	227	122	10.8	.425	-2.6	RF(50): -10.4	-0.2
2018	MIL	MLB	25	235	82	9.7	.386	-0.2	RF(55): -2.0	-0.2
2019	SEA	MLB	26	507	102	13.5	.347	0.1	LF(59): -4.2, RF(42): -3.0	0.6
2020	SEA	MLB	27	251	106	10.0	.343	-0.2	RF -3, LF 0	0.7

Domingo Santana, continued

Batted Ball Distribution

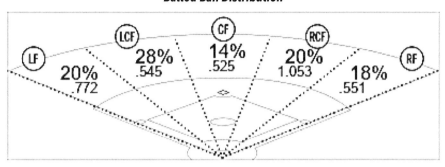

Strike Zone vs LHP   Strike Zone vs RHP

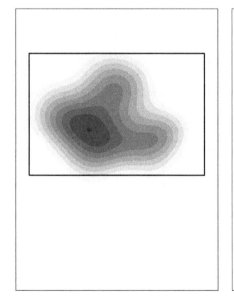
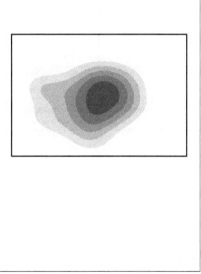

Logan Allen   LHP

Born: 05/23/97   Age: 23   Bats: R   Throws: L
Height: 6'3"   Weight: 200   Origin: Round 8, 2015 Draft (#231 overall)

YEAR	TEAM	LVL	AGE	W	L	SV	G	GS	IP	H	HR	BB/9	K/9	K	GB%	BABIP
2017	FTW	A	20	5	4	0	13	13	68^1	49	1	3.4	11.2	85	43%	.294
2017	LEL	A+	20	2	5	0	11	10	56^2	60	2	2.9	9.1	57	50%	.352
2018	SAN	AA	21	10	6	0	20	19	121	89	7	2.8	9.3	125	43%	.269
2018	ELP	AAA	21	4	0	0	5	5	27^2	21	4	4.2	8.5	26	38%	.236
2019	ELP	AAA	22	4	3	0	13	13	57^2	61	8	3.4	9.8	63	47%	.338
2019	COH	AAA	22	1	1	0	5	5	22^1	31	6	4.8	7.3	18	24%	.362
2019	SDN	MLB	22	2	3	0	8	4	25^1	33	4	4.6	5.0	14	54%	.341
2019	CLE	MLB	22	0	0	0	1	0	2^1	3	0	0.0	11.6	3	17%	.500
2020	CLE	MLB	23	5	6	0	41	11	88	99	14	3.8	6.9	68	43%	.310

Comparables: Brett Cecil, Peter Lambert, Stephen Gonsalves

Replacing an outspoken righty is always a tall task. Ask Logan Roy. Another Logan, Sr. Allen, was faced with that challenge after being acquired as part of a three-team deal that also involved Trevor Bauer and Yasiel Puig. Allen's rookie exploits didn't go well, but it could've been worse. It should get better, too. He pairs a mid-90s heater with a plus changeup and more than enough strike-throwing ability to profile as at least at No. 4 type. Cleveland has gotten more mileage than most out of that type—he just needs to cruise on the mound and not off somewhere with Waystar Royco.

YEAR	TEAM	LVL	AGE	WHIP	ERA	DRA	WARP	MPH	FB%	WHF	CSP
2017	FTW	A	20	1.10	2.11	2.52	2.2				
2017	LEL	A+	20	1.38	3.97	3.95	0.9				
2018	SAN	AA	21	1.05	2.75	3.22	3.0				
2018	ELP	AAA	21	1.23	1.63	3.24	0.7				
2019	ELP	AAA	22	1.44	5.15	3.84	1.6				
2019	COH	AAA	22	1.93	7.66	8.48	-0.4				
2019	SDN	MLB	22	1.82	6.75	6.71	-0.3	95.2	48.7	10	46.6
2019	CLE	MLB	22	1.29	0.00	8.06	-0.1	96.0	42.5	12.5	52.4
2020	CLE	MLB	23	1.54	5.47	5.39	0.1	95.2	49.8	10.6	48.8

Logan Allen, continued

Pitch Shape vs LHH   ### Pitch Shape vs RHH

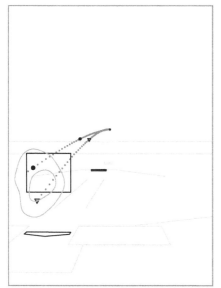 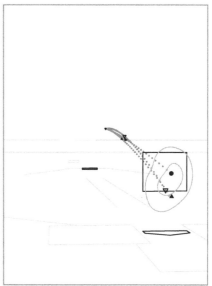

Type	Frequency	Velocity	H Movement	V Movement
● Fastball	48.1%	93 [102]	6.5 [102]	-14.4 [104]
□ Sinker				
+ Cutter				
▲ Changeup	21.2%	82.7 [91]	8.4 [113]	-30.1 [92]
✕ Splitter				
▽ Slider	23.4%	83.8 [97]	3.8 [95]	-35.1 [94]
◇ Curveball	7.3%	76.8 [94]	-7 [98]	-51.5 [92]
⊕ Slow Curveball				
✳ Knuckleball				
▼ Screwball				

Shane Bieber   RHP

Born: 05/31/95   Age: 25   Bats: R   Throws: R
Height: 6'3"   Weight: 200   Origin: Round 4, 2016 Draft (#122 overall)

YEAR	TEAM	LVL	AGE	W	L	SV	G	GS	IP	H	HR	BB/9	K/9	K	GB%	BABIP
2017	LKC	A	22	2	3	0	5	5	29	34	1	0.3	9.6	31	45%	.375
2017	LYN	A+	22	6	1	0	14	14	90	95	5	0.4	8.2	82	50%	.340
2017	AKR	AA	22	2	1	0	9	9	54¹	56	2	0.8	8.1	49	50%	.331
2018	AKR	AA	23	3	0	0	5	5	31	26	1	0.3	8.7	30	48%	.278
2018	COH	AAA	23	3	1	0	8	8	48²	30	3	1.1	8.7	47	56%	.225
2018	CLE	MLB	23	11	5	0	20	19	114²	130	13	1.8	9.3	118	46%	.356
2019	CLE	MLB	24	15	8	0	34	33	214¹	186	31	1.7	10.9	259	45%	.296
2020	CLE	MLB	25	12	8	0	29	29	178	162	24	2.2	10.8	213	45%	.310

Comparables: Danny Salazar, Joe Musgrove, Yonny Chirinos

Everyone missed on Bieber, in a sense. He was pegged as a control-over-stuff pitcher as a prospect, a fancy way of saying "potential back-end starter." Cleveland even seemed open to trading him shortly after his big-league debut, only to have at least one offer for a young outfielder rebuked. Yet Bieber added to his heater, chucked his slider a little harder and recast himself as a 200-inning ace in 2019. His finished second in the league in innings, and third in strikeouts. That's decent. Bieber even won All-Star Game MVP honors—pleasing the hometown crowd. If 2019 is any indication, Bieber might well follow in Corey Kluber's footsteps as a late-bloomer who exceeds expectations. He seems well on his way.

YEAR	TEAM	LVL	AGE	WHIP	ERA	DRA	WARP	MPH	FB%	WHF	CSP
2017	LKC	A	22	1.21	3.10	3.93	0.5				
2017	LYN	A+	22	1.10	3.10	3.99	1.3				
2017	AKR	AA	22	1.12	2.32	3.49	1.1				
2018	AKR	AA	23	0.87	1.16	2.40	1.1				
2018	COH	AAA	23	0.74	1.66	2.30	1.8				
2018	CLE	MLB	23	1.33	4.55	3.32	2.6	94.8	57.4	12.3	51.2
2019	CLE	MLB	24	1.05	3.28	3.68	4.9	94.6	45.8	14.7	45.1
2020	CLE	MLB	25	1.16	3.26	3.60	3.9	94.4	50.5	14.3	49

Shane Bieber, continued

Pitch Shape vs LHH

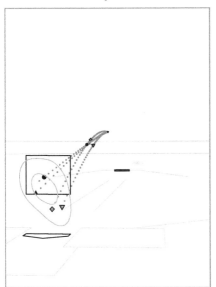

Pitch Shape vs RHH

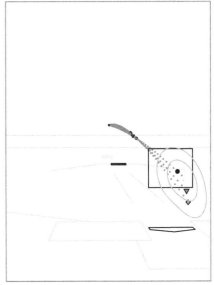

Type	Frequency	Velocity	H Movement	V Movement
● Fastball	45.7%	93.4 [103]	-7.3 [98]	-12.3 [110]
☐ Sinker				
+ Cutter				
▲ Changeup	7.3%	87.9 [110]	-13.9 [87]	-25.4 [106]
✕ Splitter				
▽ Slider	26.5%	85.3 [104]	1.4 [85]	-30.8 [107]
◇ Curveball	20.4%	82.9 [114]	3.7 [85]	-44.7 [106]
✦ Slow Curveball				
✳ Knuckleball				
▼ Screwball				

Carlos Carrasco   RHP

Born: 03/21/87   Age: 33   Bats: R   Throws: R
Height: 6'4"   Weight: 224   Origin: International Free Agent, 2003

YEAR	TEAM	LVL	AGE	W	L	SV	G	GS	IP	H	HR	BB/9	K/9	K	GB%	BABIP
2017	CLE	MLB	30	18	6	0	32	32	200	173	21	2.1	10.2	226	47%	.307
2018	CLE	MLB	31	17	10	0	32	30	192	173	21	2.0	10.8	231	48%	.315
2019	CLE	MLB	32	6	7	1	23	12	80	92	18	1.8	10.8	96	42%	.354
2020	*CLE*	*MLB*	*33*	*9*	*6*	*0*	*23*	*23*	*129*	*119*	*18*	*2.3*	*10.6*	*153*	*45%*	*.308*

Comparables: Curt Schilling, Michael Bowden, Collin McHugh

It's not always about baseball; in fact, it shouldn't be. After sputtering to start the year, Carrasco complained of sluggishness and fatigue—something just wasn't right. He was subsequently shut down in late May, due to a blood condition that was later revealed to be leukemia. His early-season struggles were placed in perspective as he entered his next battle, with a more fearsome foe than big-league hitters.

In July, MLB featured Carrasco as part of the All-Star festivities in Cleveland, where the hometown fans and the baseball world, as well as humans with heart could show their support during the All-Star Game's annual "Stand Up to Cancer" showcase in a fitting tribute to a beloved teammate and player. Awards are generally silly, but Carrasco's humanitarianism earned him the 2019 Roberto Clemente Award, an honor bestowed upon the player that "best exemplifies the game of baseball, sportsmanship, community involvement and the individual's contribution to his team." It's hard to imagine a more suitable champion for the cause. To wit, Carrasco spent time during his recovery helping underprivileged families in need.

On a more trivial note, Carrasco was even able to follow through on his promise to return to the bump in 2019, hitting 99 mph on the gun with regularity in a handful of September relief appearances. It wasn't vintage Carrasco by any stretch, as he had spotty control and struggled to keep the ball in the yard—in retrospect giving high-leverage, playoff-chasing innings to someone who had been preoccupied with fighting for his life may have not been the best strategy—but that's hardly the point.

It's difficult to predict his 2020 outlook with any certainty, but it doesn't really matter, because it's not always about baseball, and Carrasco's 2019 season can only be considered a rousing triumph.

YEAR	TEAM	LVL	AGE	WHIP	ERA	DRA	WARP	MPH	FB%	WHF	CSP
2017	CLE	MLB	30	1.10	3.29	2.79	6.2	96.7	48.9	14.5	47.5
2018	CLE	MLB	31	1.12	3.38	2.91	5.3	95.8	44.9	16.5	45.9
2019	CLE	MLB	32	1.35	5.29	5.44	0.2	96.0	46	16.2	46.4
2020	CLE	MLB	33	1.18	3.46	3.78	2.6	95.1	45.9	15.6	46

Carlos Carrasco, continued

Pitch Shape vs LHH

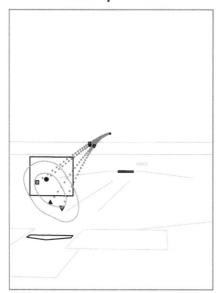

Pitch Shape vs RHH

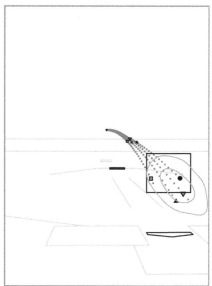

Type		Frequency	Velocity	H Movement	V Movement
●	Fastball	33.8%	94.2 [105]	-10.2 [85]	-15.2 [102]
□	Sinker	12.2%	93 [102]	-14.6 [87]	-20.8 [99]
+	Cutter				
▲	Changeup	18.4%	88.2 [111]	-8.4 [113]	-30.7 [90]
✕	Splitter				
▽	Slider	32.4%	85.2 [103]	2.3 [89]	-34 [97]
◇	Curveball	3.3%	82.7 [114]	6.5 [96]	-41.2 [113]
⊕	Slow Curveball				
✳	Knuckleball				
▼	Screwball				

Adam Cimber RHP

Born: 08/15/90   Age: 29   Bats: R   Throws: R
Height: 6'4"   Weight: 195   Origin: Round 9, 2013 Draft (#268 overall)

YEAR	TEAM	LVL	AGE	W	L	SV	G	GS	IP	H	HR	BB/9	K/9	K	GB%	BABIP
2017	SAN	AA	26	1	1	1	12	0	16	12	1	1.1	7.3	13	48%	.244
2017	ELP	AAA	26	4	1	4	37	2	64²	51	10	1.1	7.2	52	55%	.233
2018	SDN	MLB	27	3	5	0	42	0	48¹	42	2	1.9	9.5	51	53%	.315
2018	CLE	MLB	27	0	3	0	28	0	20	26	3	3.2	3.2	7	68%	.324
2019	CLE	MLB	28	6	3	1	68	0	56²	56	6	3.0	6.5	41	56%	.287
2020	CLE	MLB	29	3	3	2	55	0	58	64	12	2.3	6.7	43	55%	.290

Comparables: Chasen Bradford, Nick Wittgren, Robby Scott

If you're playing limbo, don't invite Cimber. If you're in an argument, be careful—Cimber won't take the high road. If you find low-hanging fruit delicious, you better pick it quickly because…well, you get it. The other reliever acquired in the Brad Hand-Francisco Mejía trade, Cimber has overcome a mediocre strikeout rate to become a trusted high-leverage specialist. Just don't ask him to grab something off the top shelf—or face a left-handed batter.

YEAR	TEAM	LVL	AGE	WHIP	ERA	DRA	WARP	MPH	FB%	WHF	CSP
2017	SAN	AA	26	0.88	2.81	3.26	0.3				
2017	ELP	AAA	26	0.91	2.92	1.99	2.4				
2018	SDN	MLB	27	1.08	3.17	3.92	0.6	89.2	75.8	12.7	59.1
2018	CLE	MLB	27	1.65	4.05	6.17	-0.3	89.4	73.5	7.4	50.4
2019	CLE	MLB	28	1.32	4.45	5.26	0.1	88.0	67.8	10.3	49.7
2020	CLE	MLB	29	1.35	4.97	5.15	0.0	88.0	71.3	10.6	52.6

Adam Cimber, continued

Pitch Shape vs LHH	Pitch Shape vs RHH

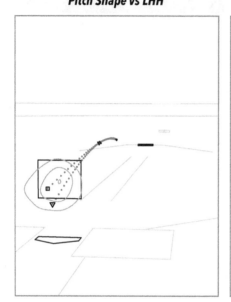 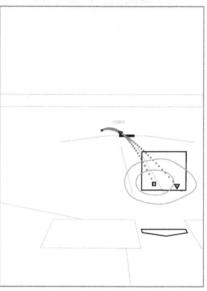

Type	Frequency	Velocity	H Movement	V Movement
● Fastball				
☐ Sinker	67.8%	85.5 [63]	-12.6 [101]	-39.4 [33]
+ Cutter				
▲ Changeup				
✕ Splitter				
▽ Slider	32.2%	75.7 [63]	5 [100]	-40.8 [78]
◇ Curveball				
✦ Slow Curveball				
✳ Knuckleball				
▼ Screwball				

Aaron Civale   RHP

Born: 06/12/95   Age: 25   Bats: R   Throws: R
Height: 6'2"   Weight: 215   Origin: Round 3, 2016 Draft (#92 overall)

YEAR	TEAM	LVL	AGE	W	L	SV	G	GS	IP	H	HR	BB/9	K/9	K	GB%	BABIP
2017	LKC	A	22	2	4	0	10	10	57	64	2	0.8	8.4	53	55%	.358
2017	LYN	A+	22	11	2	0	17	17	107²	96	11	0.8	7.4	88	49%	.276
2018	AKR	AA	23	5	7	0	21	21	106¹	115	12	1.8	6.6	78	49%	.308
2019	AKR	AA	24	4	0	0	5	5	30¹	26	3	1.8	7.1	24	42%	.264
2019	COH	AAA	24	3	1	0	8	8	42¹	38	4	1.9	9.8	46	40%	.296
2019	CLE	MLB	24	3	4	0	10	10	57²	44	4	2.5	7.2	46	42%	.250
2020	CLE	MLB	25	8	7	0	23	23	125	126	21	3.0	7.3	102	42%	.286

Comparables: Tyler Wilson, Anthony DeSclafani, Dario Agrazal

Civale went 10 starts before giving up more than two earned runs in an outing, but he didn't truly enter the zeitgeist until an umpire tweeted a poorly spelled attempt at "civil." Ah, well. While Civale might not have been anyone's first choice to help prop up a patchwork rotation, he led Cleveland's starters in ERA. How? By leaning heavily on an über-spinny breaking ball and a keen knack for evading loud contact. Whether or not that proves sustainable, Civale has displayed a stinginess on baserunners via the walk, which should help keep him in the mix as a back-end starter for the foreseeable future.

YEAR	TEAM	LVL	AGE	WHIP	ERA	DRA	WARP	MPH	FB%	WHF	CSP
2017	LKC	A	22	1.21	4.58	4.73	0.4				
2017	LYN	A+	22	0.98	2.59	3.53	2.2				
2018	AKR	AA	23	1.28	3.89	5.03	0.4				
2019	AKR	AA	24	1.05	2.67	4.88	0.0				
2019	COH	AAA	24	1.11	2.13	3.01	1.5				
2019	CLE	MLB	24	1.04	2.34	5.13	0.4	94.1	38.5	9.7	41.8
2020	CLE	MLB	25	1.34	4.43	4.64	1.3	93.8	39.5	9.9	42.8

Aaron Civale, continued

Pitch Shape vs LHH
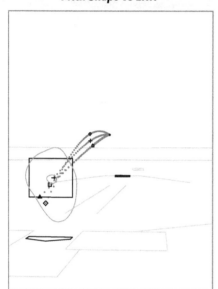

Pitch Shape vs RHH
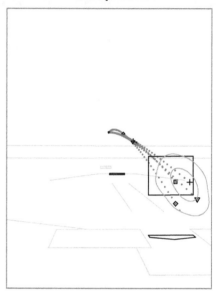

Type	Frequency	Velocity	H Movement	V Movement
● Fastball	3.1%	92.1 [99]	-4 [113]	-14.6 [104]
□ Sinker	35.4%	92.6 [100]	-12.4 [102]	-19 [105]
+ Cutter	28.8%	87.9 [95]	4.8 [117]	-23.5 [102]
▲ Changeup	6.5%	84.2 [96]	-13.6 [88]	-26 [104]
✕ Splitter				
▽ Slider	15.1%	83.6 [97]	8.8 [116]	-33 [100]
◇ Curveball	11.1%	75.4 [89]	11.3 [115]	-58.5 [77]
⊕ Slow Curveball				
✳ Knuckleball				
▼ Screwball				

Emmanuel Clase   RHP

Born: 03/18/98   Age: 22   Bats: R   Throws: R
Height: 6'2"   Weight: 206   Origin: International Free Agent, 2015

YEAR	TEAM	LVL	AGE	W	L	SV	G	GS	IP	H	HR	BB/9	K/9	K	GB%	BABIP
2017	SDP	RK	19	2	4	0	9	6	35^2	40	4	5.6	10.6	42	48%	.360
2018	SPO	A-	20	1	1	12	22	0	28^1	16	0	1.9	8.6	27	62%	.222
2019	DEB	A+	21	2	0	1	6	0	7	4	0	1.3	14.1	11	77%	.308
2019	FRI	AA	21	1	2	11	33	1	37^2	34	1	1.9	9.3	39	62%	.314
2019	TEX	MLB	21	2	3	1	21	1	23^1	20	2	2.3	8.1	21	59%	.281
2020	*CLE*	*MLB*	*22*	*2*	*2*	*4*	*45*	*0*	*48*	*46*	*7*	*3.5*	*8.8*	*47*	*55%*	*.296*

Comparables: Yennsy Diaz, Jake Newberry, Michael Feliz

Question: how did Clase learn to throw a 102 mph cutter? Allow us to answer your question with a question: How did Beethoven learn to compose melody? How did Superman learn to fly? How did Elvis Presley learn to do that thing with his hips? How did Bob Beamon learn to… also fly? How did Jason Giambi learn to apply hair gel? How did that one lady from the memes learn to make her eyes pop out like that? How did shows like NCIS or Criminal Minds or House become so popular despite having more or less the exact same plot every week? What we're saying here is that an answer definitely exists, but we remain unconvinced that knowing the answer at the expense of the mystery would add to the enjoyment in any material way. Another mystery: will Emmanuel Clase…close? (that pun only works in print; Clase is pronounced Clah-SAY, so if you say it out loud, you have to say it like "will Clah-SAY … CLOH-ZAY?!" and you have to make dad-joke face when you do it.)

YEAR	TEAM	LVL	AGE	WHIP	ERA	DRA	WARP	MPH	FB%	WHF	CSP
2017	SDP	RK	19	1.74	5.30	6.12	-0.1				
2018	SPO	A-	20	0.78	0.64	2.25	0.9				
2019	DEB	A+	21	0.71	0.00	2.98	0.1				
2019	FRI	AA	21	1.12	3.35	3.70	0.4				
2019	TEX	MLB	21	1.11	2.31	3.91	0.4	101.1	78.8	12.2	49.4
2020	*CLE*	*MLB*	*22*	*1.34*	*4.09*	*4.29*	*0.5*	*101.1*	*82.2*	*12.7*	*51.5*

Emmanuel Clase, continued

Pitch Shape vs LHH

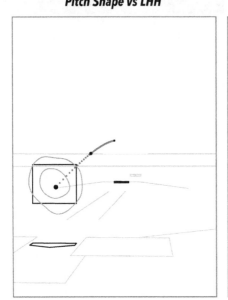

Pitch Shape vs RHH

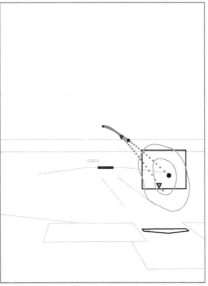

Type	Frequency	Velocity	H Movement	V Movement
● Fastball	78.8%	99.4 [120]	1.4 [137]	-15.7 [101]
□ Sinker				
+ Cutter				
▲ Changeup				
✕ Splitter				
▽ Slider	21.2%	90.6 [126]	4.1 [96]	-32.4 [102]
◇ Curveball				
⬥ Slow Curveball				
✳ Knuckleball				
▼ Screwball				

Mike Clevinger   RHP

Born: 12/21/90   Age: 29   Bats: R   Throws: R
Height: 6'4"   Weight: 215   Origin: Round 4, 2011 Draft (#135 overall)

YEAR	TEAM	LVL	AGE	W	L	SV	G	GS	IP	H	HR	BB/9	K/9	K	GB%	BABIP
2017	COH	AAA	26	3	2	0	7	7	34	28	3	3.7	10.1	38	40%	.298
2017	CLE	MLB	26	12	6	0	27	21	121²	92	13	4.4	10.1	137	40%	.274
2018	CLE	MLB	27	13	8	0	32	32	200	164	21	3.0	9.3	207	41%	.280
2019	CLE	MLB	28	13	4	0	21	21	126	96	10	2.6	12.1	169	41%	.306
2020	CLE	MLB	29	11	8	0	28	28	162	136	21	3.7	12.1	219	42%	.308

Comparables: Domingo Germán, Mike Hauschild, Chad Green

To paraphrase Led Zeppelin, Cleveland sings loud for the sunshine while their opponents pray hard for the rain. Clevinger had his finest season as a big-leaguer, twirling 99-mph heaters and swing-and-miss sliders; setting new career-bests in ERA and strikeout-to-walk ratio. The only blemish was the fact he was limited to 21 starts due to a pair of trips to the injured list: once for a sprained ankle, another for a strained back. Otherwise? Nary a cloud in the sky.

YEAR	TEAM	LVL	AGE	WHIP	ERA	DRA	WARP	MPH	FB%	WHF	CSP
2017	COH	AAA	26	1.24	2.65	3.48	0.8				
2017	CLE	MLB	26	1.25	3.11	3.61	2.6	94.7	53.5	13.1	42.7
2018	CLE	MLB	27	1.15	3.02	3.52	4.1	96.2	52.9	12.8	48.8
2019	CLE	MLB	28	1.06	2.71	3.32	3.3	97.7	51.2	16.1	45.9
2020	CLE	MLB	29	1.24	3.34	3.57	3.6	95.7	52.4	14	46.1

Cleveland Indians 2020

Mike Clevinger, continued

Pitch Shape vs LHH

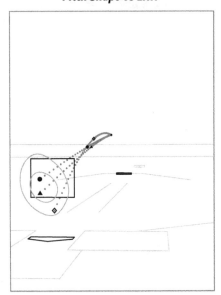

Pitch Shape vs RHH

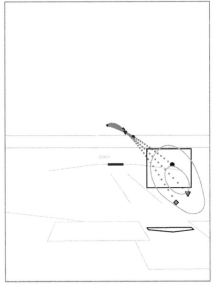

Type	Frequency	Velocity	H Movement	V Movement
● Fastball	51.1%	95.6 [109]	-4.7 [110]	-10.9 [113]
☐ Sinker				
+ Cutter				
▲ Changeup	11.3%	87.3 [107]	-10.4 [104]	-21.9 [116]
✕ Splitter				
▽ Slider	25.6%	80.9 [85]	15.2 [143]	-38.8 [83]
◇ Curveball	12.0%	77.8 [97]	7.8 [101]	-52.2 [90]
◈ Slow Curveball				
✳ Knuckleball				
▼ Screwball				

Brad Hand LHP

Born: 03/20/90   Age: 30   Bats: L   Throws: L
Height: 6'3"   Weight: 220   Origin: Round 2, 2008 Draft (#52 overall)

YEAR	TEAM	LVL	AGE	W	L	SV	G	GS	IP	H	HR	BB/9	K/9	K	GB%	BABIP
2017	SDN	MLB	27	3	4	21	72	0	79¹	54	9	2.3	11.8	104	46%	.263
2018	SDN	MLB	28	2	4	24	41	0	44¹	33	5	3.0	13.2	65	48%	.298
2018	CLE	MLB	28	0	1	8	28	0	27²	19	3	4.2	13.3	41	44%	.286
2019	CLE	MLB	29	6	4	34	60	0	57¹	53	6	2.8	13.2	84	28%	.362
2020	CLE	MLB	30	3	3	34	55	0	58	51	9	3.2	12.0	78	36%	.310

Comparables: Randall Delgado, Brett Cecil, Drew Pomeranz

In July 2018, Cleveland pondered, "How do we get the hand?" Just once in their existence, they wanted hand—but they had no hand. No hand at all. And let us tell you something, a team without a hand is not a team. Upon acquiring Hand, the team enjoyed a few months of dominant relief work and seemed set at closer for a few seasons longer. Cleveland enjoyed Hand through the first half of 2019, too, as he punched out 55 batters in 37 innings of work en route to his third consecutive All-Star Game appearance. Cleveland had so much hand, they were coming out of their gloves. The second half, however, was far less kind. The strikeout numbers remained lofty, but his walk rate shot up. Hand also served up twice as many dingers in the second half than the first half—despite having thrown nearly half as many innings—and hitters slashed .310/.383/.512 against him. (Yoán Moncada hit .315/.367/.548, for reference.) Hand was then limited to two appearances in Cleveland's last 20 appearances due to arm fatigue. He has up to two years remaining of team control, but for the first time in a while there's reason for skepticism about what those seasons will entail.

YEAR	TEAM	LVL	AGE	WHIP	ERA	DRA	WARP	MPH	FB%	WHF	CSP
2017	SDN	MLB	27	0.93	2.16	3.03	1.9	95.5	51.1	14.1	46.1
2018	SDN	MLB	28	1.08	3.05	3.15	0.9	96.4	44.2	13.6	50
2018	CLE	MLB	28	1.16	2.28	3.47	0.5	95.7	48.1	13.2	52.7
2019	CLE	MLB	29	1.24	3.30	4.24	0.7	95.0	45.8	14.6	49.6
2020	CLE	MLB	30	1.22	3.58	3.84	0.9	94.8	47.1	14	49

Brad Hand, continued

Pitch Shape vs LHH

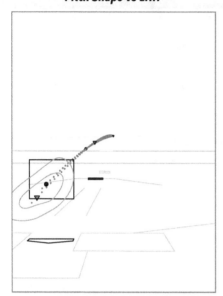

Pitch Shape vs RHH

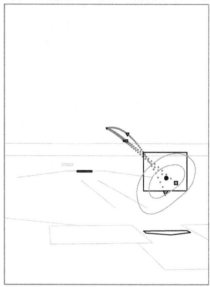

Type		Frequency	Velocity	H Movement	V Movement
●	Fastball	41.8%	92.9 [101]	9.8 [87]	-14.9 [103]
□	Sinker	4.0%	91.9 [96]	13.7 [93]	-20.3 [100]
+	Cutter				
▲	Changeup				
✕	Splitter				
▽	Slider	54.2%	81.2 [87]	-13.2 [134]	-38.4 [85]
◇	Curveball				
✦	Slow Curveball				
✳	Knuckleball				
▼	Screwball				

Zach Plesac RHP

Born: 01/21/95   Age: 25   Bats: R   Throws: R
Height: 6'3"   Weight: 220   Origin: Round 12, 2016 Draft (#362 overall)

YEAR	TEAM	LVL	AGE	W	L	SV	G	GS	IP	H	HR	BB/9	K/9	K	GB%	BABIP
2017	MHV	A-	22	0	1	0	8	7	26	14	0	2.8	10.7	31	46%	.246
2017	LKC	A	22	1	1	0	6	6	25	19	2	2.2	6.8	19	38%	.236
2018	LYN	A+	23	8	5	0	22	22	122²	124	8	2.4	8.1	111	45%	.327
2018	AKR	AA	23	3	1	0	4	4	22	19	1	1.6	8.6	21	30%	.300
2019	AKR	AA	24	1	1	0	6	6	37¹	23	0	1.4	8.2	34	50%	.237
2019	COH	AAA	24	3	1	0	4	4	26¹	19	2	1.0	10.6	31	31%	.270
2019	CLE	MLB	24	8	6	0	21	21	115²	102	19	3.1	6.8	88	40%	.255
2020	CLE	MLB	25	8	8	0	33	23	133	131	23	3.0	7.1	105	39%	.278

Comparables: Michael King, Erick Fedde, Tyler Duffey

In an ode to fellow Ball State University alumnus David Letterman, we were going to present the top 10 fun facts about Plesac's rookie year. Space limitations and self-respect led us to cut it down to three. Let's go. No. 1: Despite being thought of as a fastball-changeup pitcher coming up, the righty's slider generated his best whiff rate. No. 2: This is his first Annual appearance, in his fourth attempt. And No. 3: Yes, he's still Dan's nephew. This was nothing less than what it was. Pretend we just threw a pencil.

YEAR	TEAM	LVL	AGE	WHIP	ERA	DRA	WARP	MPH	FB%	WHF	CSP
2017	MHV	A-	22	0.85	1.38	2.53	0.8				
2017	LKC	A	22	1.00	3.60	3.84	0.4				
2018	LYN	A+	23	1.28	4.04	4.34	1.4				
2018	AKR	AA	23	1.05	2.45	3.44	0.5				
2019	AKR	AA	24	0.78	0.96	2.58	1.1				
2019	COH	AAA	24	0.84	2.73	2.31	1.1				
2019	CLE	MLB	24	1.23	3.81	6.29	-0.6	95.7	50.6	10.3	49.8
2020	CLE	MLB	25	1.32	4.39	4.59	1.4	95.4	51.8	10.5	51

Zach Plesac, continued

Pitch Shape vs LHH

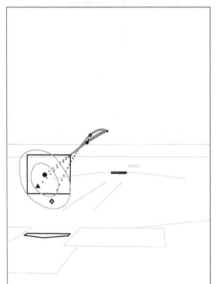

Pitch Shape vs RHH

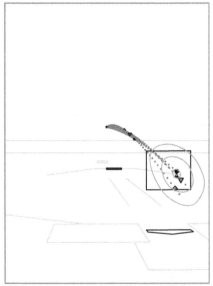

Type	Frequency	Velocity	H Movement	V Movement
● Fastball	50.6%	94.1 [105]	-8.1 [95]	-13 [108]
□ Sinker				
+ Cutter				
▲ Changeup	20.6%	86.1 [103]	-9.5 [108]	-24.5 [109]
✕ Splitter				
▽ Slider	18.8%	85.1 [103]	1.7 [86]	-30.7 [107]
◇ Curveball	10.0%	79.5 [103]	6.6 [96]	-47.5 [100]
⊕ Slow Curveball				
✱ Knuckleball				
▼ Screwball				

Oliver Pérez   LHP

Born: 08/15/81   Age: 38   Bats: L   Throws: L
Height: 6'3"   Weight: 225   Origin: International Free Agent, 1999

YEAR	TEAM	LVL	AGE	W	L	SV	G	GS	IP	H	HR	BB/9	K/9	K	GB%	BABIP
2017	WAS	MLB	35	0	0	1	50	0	33	32	4	3.3	10.6	39	32%	.333
2018	SWB	AAA	36	1	0	0	16	0	14	17	1	1.9	9.6	15	33%	.421
2018	CLE	MLB	36	1	1	0	51	0	32¹	17	1	1.9	12.0	43	46%	.239
2019	CLE	MLB	37	2	4	1	67	0	40²	38	5	2.7	10.6	48	46%	.314
2020	CLE	MLB	38	2	2	0	45	0	48	38	6	2.7	10.4	55	40%	.274

Comparables: Al Leiter, Francisco Liriano, Scott Kazmir

On October 23, 2001, Apple revolutionized the music industry—and, probably, the world—when the company released the first generation of the iPod. Pérez made his big-league debut eight months later. In the 18-plus years since, the two have appeared linked in some way. He had a "classic" run as a hotshot young starter; he "shuffled" around after repeated failure; and so on. Since 2012, he's had his "mini" phase as a left-handed specialist—an effective one, too; the kind left-handed hitters' moms warn them about. So solid is Pérez that Cleveland permitted his option to vest despite impending rule changes devaluing LOOGY. Much like the iPod you gifted your younger sibling, Pérez has survived a lot to get here—but he still works.

YEAR	TEAM	LVL	AGE	WHIP	ERA	DRA	WARP	MPH	FB%	WHF	CSP
2017	WAS	MLB	35	1.33	4.64	6.18	-0.4	94.8	57.3	11	53.6
2018	SWB	AAA	36	1.43	2.57	5.58	-0.1				
2018	CLE	MLB	36	0.74	1.39	2.61	0.9	94.1	50.9	16	52.2
2019	CLE	MLB	37	1.23	3.98	4.28	0.5	94.2	51	13.8	51.5
2020	CLE	MLB	38	1.10	3.01	3.36	1.0	92.8	51.2	13.3	50.9

Oliver Pérez, continued

Pitch Shape vs LHH	Pitch Shape vs RHH

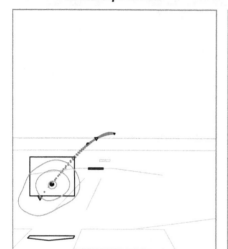 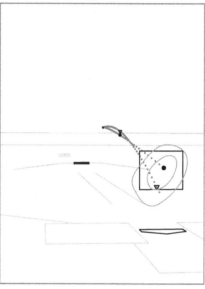

Type	Frequency	Velocity	H Movement	V Movement
● Fastball	49.6%	92 [99]	14.3 [67]	-20.7 [87]
☐ Sinker				
+ Cutter				
▲ Changeup				
✕ Splitter				
▽ Slider	48.5%	78.7 [76]	-7.6 [111]	-40.1 [80]
◇ Curveball				
◈ Slow Curveball				
✳ Knuckleball				
▼ Screwball				

Jefry Rodriguez   RHP

Born: 07/26/93   Age: 26   Bats: R   Throws: R
Height: 6'6"   Weight: 232   Origin: International Free Agent, 2012

YEAR	TEAM	LVL	AGE	W	L	SV	G	GS	IP	H	HR	BB/9	K/9	K	GB%	BABIP
2017	POT	A+	23	4	3	0	12	10	57	44	2	3.0	8.1	51	53%	.278
2018	HAR	AA	24	5	3	0	13	13	68	55	6	3.7	9.5	72	53%	.280
2018	SYR	AAA	24	2	2	0	6	6	32²	32	0	4.1	8.3	30	47%	.333
2018	WAS	MLB	24	3	3	0	14	8	52	43	8	6.4	6.8	39	46%	.240
2019	COH	AAA	25	1	0	0	5	3	21²	16	1	4.6	6.6	16	54%	.250
2019	CLE	MLB	25	1	5	0	10	8	46²	48	5	4.1	6.4	33	49%	.299
2020	CLE	MLB	26	3	4	0	37	6	64	68	11	4.3	6.7	48	48%	.294

Comparables: Elvin Ramirez, Michael Blazek, Brad Peacock

Rodriguez was the first line of defense after Cleveland's rotation was chomped by the injury bug. He started eight games before succumbing to his own malady, a strained shoulder that sidelined him for most of the summer. The highlight of his year was likely his first three-start stretch where he gave up just five runs in 18 2/3 innings against the Royals, Marlins and White Sox—it's clear that he can succeed against Triple-A talent, is what we're saying. Rodriguez is likely to end up in the bullpen once he reaches the majors on a full-time basis due to a thin arsenal and a thinner feel for throwing quality strikes.

YEAR	TEAM	LVL	AGE	WHIP	ERA	DRA	WARP	MPH	FB%	WHF	CSP
2017	POT	A+	23	1.11	3.32	3.38	1.3				
2018	HAR	AA	24	1.22	3.31	3.62	1.4				
2018	SYR	AAA	24	1.44	3.58	4.56	0.4				
2018	WAS	MLB	24	1.54	5.71	7.35	-1.3	97.8	65	9.2	46.1
2019	COH	AAA	25	1.25	4.15	4.21	0.5				
2019	CLE	MLB	25	1.48	4.63	7.00	-0.6	96.7	70	8.7	46.9
2020	CLE	MLB	26	1.55	5.38	5.31	0.1	96.8	68.8	9.1	47.4

Jefry Rodriguez, continued

Pitch Shape vs LHH

Pitch Shape vs RHH

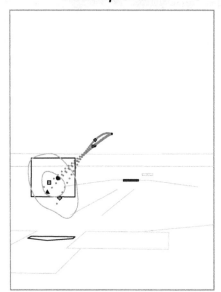 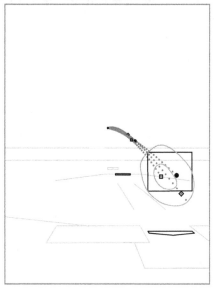

Type	Frequency	Velocity	H Movement	V Movement
● Fastball	28.0%	94.5 [106]	-7.4 [98]	-12.6 [109]
□ Sinker	42.0%	93.8 [106]	-13.4 [95]	-17.3 [111]
+ Cutter				
▲ Changeup	7.0%	88.3 [111]	-12.4 [94]	-23.9 [110]
✕ Splitter				
▽ Slider				
◇ Curveball	23.0%	81.5 [109]	4.9 [90]	-40.4 [115]
⊕ Slow Curveball				
✳ Knuckleball				
▼ Screwball				

Nick Wittgren   RHP

Born: 05/29/91   Age: 29   Bats: R   Throws: R
Height: 6'2"   Weight: 216   Origin: Round 9, 2012 Draft (#287 overall)

YEAR	TEAM	LVL	AGE	W	L	SV	G	GS	IP	H	HR	BB/9	K/9	K	GB%	BABIP
2017	MIA	MLB	26	3	1	0	38	0	42¹	46	5	2.8	9.1	43	32%	.339
2018	NWO	AAA	27	0	5	2	25	0	29¹	34	4	2.5	10.4	34	46%	.353
2018	MIA	MLB	27	2	1	0	32	0	33²	29	1	4.0	8.3	31	46%	.280
2019	CLE	MLB	28	5	1	4	55	0	57²	47	10	2.3	9.4	60	40%	.253
2020	CLE	MLB	29	3	3	2	55	0	58	55	9	2.8	8.6	56	39%	.287

Comparables: Chase Whitley, Preston Guilmet, Evan Scribner

Cleveland pulled a neat trick last February when it convinced the Marlins to take Jordan Milbrath in exchange for Wittgren. Why Miami agreed to the deal is beyond us. Milbrath is about 60 days younger, and has zero big-league experience to his credit. Conversely, Wittgren has now accumulated 185 innings of quality relief work. Sure, he's not impressive to watch—he mostly spams the opposition with his low-90s fastball—but there's something to be said about valuing results to aesthetics, especially when those results come this cheap.

YEAR	TEAM	LVL	AGE	WHIP	ERA	DRA	WARP	MPH	FB%	WHF	CSP
2017	MIA	MLB	26	1.39	4.68	4.40	0.4	94.4	72.8	12	52.5
2018	NWO	AAA	27	1.43	5.22	4.24	0.3				
2018	MIA	MLB	27	1.31	2.94	3.81	0.4	94.4	70	10.7	49
2019	CLE	MLB	28	1.08	2.81	4.91	0.3	94.2	66.4	10.8	48.6
2020	CLE	MLB	29	1.26	3.89	4.13	0.7	93.6	68.8	11.1	49.7

Nick Wittgren, continued

Pitch Shape vs LHH

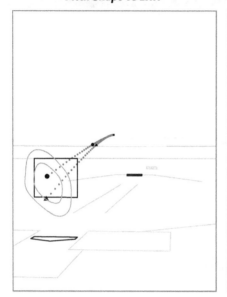

Pitch Shape vs RHH

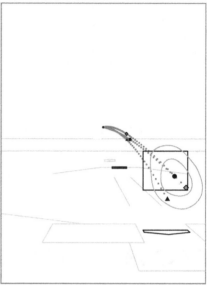

Type		Frequency	Velocity	H Movement	V Movement
●	Fastball	66.4%	92.7 [101]	-7 [99]	-14 [105]
□	Sinker				
+	Cutter				
▲	Changeup	14.6%	85.9 [102]	-11.9 [97]	-30.2 [92]
×	Splitter				
▽	Slider				
◇	Curveball	19.0%	83.9 [117]	4.7 [89]	-35.9 [125]
⊕	Slow Curveball				
✳	Knuckleball				
▼	Screwball				

Hunter Wood   RHP

Born: 08/12/93   Age: 26   Bats: R   Throws: R
Height: 6'1"   Weight: 175   Origin: Round 29, 2013 Draft (#878 overall)

YEAR	TEAM	LVL	AGE	W	L	SV	G	GS	IP	H	HR	BB/9	K/9	K	GB%	BABIP
2017	MNT	AA	23	4	4	0	12	12	70	68	7	3.1	8.7	68	38%	.319
2017	DUR	AAA	23	3	1	0	19	6	53¹	54	8	3.4	7.9	47	46%	.299
2017	TBA	MLB	23	0	0	0	1	0	0¹	0	0	0.0	0.0	0	0%	.000
2018	DUR	AAA	24	2	2	3	24	2	42	26	4	2.1	13.5	63	46%	.262
2018	TBA	MLB	24	1	1	0	29	8	41	42	4	4.0	9.2	42	44%	.330
2019	DUR	AAA	25	1	0	1	8	0	10²	16	3	4.2	11.8	14	26%	.419
2019	CLE	MLB	25	0	0	0	17	0	16¹	20	3	2.8	8.3	15	38%	.327
2019	TBA	MLB	25	1	1	1	19	2	29	26	4	2.2	7.4	24	31%	.265
2020	CLE	MLB	26	2	2	0	40	0	42	42	8	3.3	8.9	42	35%	.292

Comparables: John Gant, Nick Tropeano, Luis Cessa

Wood is similar to Wittgren in two regards: 1) his results also don't match his aesthetics; and 2) he too was acquired for pennies from a Florida-based team. Both fit in fine, as Cleveland's bullpen finished third in ERA and last in average fastball velocity. It's worth wondering if there's a connection there. Velocity matters—we're not suggesting otherwise—but there are bargains to be had if teams are going to approach every low-to-mid-90s hurler with the indifference that the Rays and Marlins had toward Wood and Wittgren. Luck is said to be the residue of design, so credit Cleveland for being there to take advantage of other teams' biases.

YEAR	TEAM	LVL	AGE	WHIP	ERA	DRA	WARP	MPH	FB%	WHF	CSP
2017	MNT	AA	23	1.31	4.76	4.66	0.4				
2017	DUR	AAA	23	1.39	4.39	5.25	0.2				
2017	TBA	MLB	23	0.00	0.00	4.12	0.0	89.9	40	0	38.2
2018	DUR	AAA	24	0.86	3.00	2.44	1.3				
2018	TBA	MLB	24	1.46	3.73	2.97	1.0	96.5	52.7	14.4	45.6
2019	DUR	AAA	25	1.97	7.59	6.25	0.0				
2019	CLE	MLB	25	1.53	3.86	4.32	0.2	95.7	58.9	13	39.9
2019	TBA	MLB	25	1.14	2.48	6.59	-0.4	95.3	58.9	12.5	48
2020	CLE	MLB	26	1.35	4.56	4.73	0.2	95.5	57.2	13.6	44.3

Hunter Wood, continued

Pitch Shape vs LHH

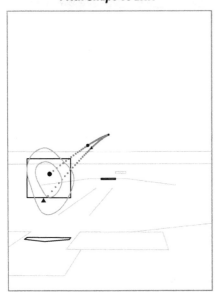

Pitch Shape vs RHH

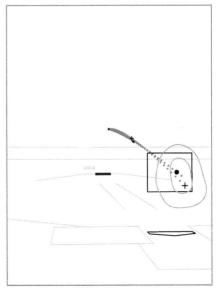

Type	Frequency	Velocity	H Movement	V Movement
● Fastball	56.0%	93.9 [104]	-1.1 [126]	-10.8 [113]
□ Sinker				
+ Cutter	27.6%	86.8 [88]	5.7 [123]	-28.5 [84]
▲ Changeup	11.3%	86.5 [105]	-9.3 [109]	-21.6 [117]
✕ Splitter				
▽ Slider				
◇ Curveball	5.1%	76.8 [94]	7 [98]	-54.3 [86]
⊕ Slow Curveball				
✱ Knuckleball				
▼ Screwball				

PLAYER COMMENTS WITHOUT GRAPHS

Will Benson   OF

Born: 06/16/98   Age: 22   Bats: L   Throws: L
Height: 6'5"   Weight: 225   Origin: Round 1, 2016 Draft (#14 overall)

YEAR	TEAM	LVL	AGE	PA	R	2B	3B	HR	RBI	BB	K	SB	CS	AVG/OBP/SLG
2017	MHV	A-	19	236	29	8	5	10	36	31	80	7	1	.238/.347/.475
2018	LKC	A	20	506	54	11	1	22	58	82	152	12	6	.180/.324/.370
2019	LKC	A	21	259	44	12	3	18	55	37	78	18	2	.272/.371/.604
2019	LYN	A+	21	255	29	9	2	4	23	31	73	9	2	.189/.290/.304
2020	CLE	MLB	22	251	23	10	1	7	26	21	94	2	1	.180/.253/.332

Comparables: Jamie Romak, Derek Norris, Tommy Pham

Sometimes potential and promise can be a double-edged sword. The first season of HBO's *Game of Thrones* (ever heard of it?) peaked with over three million U.S. viewers, garnering rave reviews both critically and commercially. The sky was the limit for the fantasy series, and by the eighth and final season, almost 14 million Americans were glued to the television, awaiting the fate of Westeros. Then it ended, and all the hope for an epic finish was dashed by a rushed, careless finale. Anyway, Will Benson was drafted in the first round, with his scouting reports brimming with glowing descriptors about his tools, projection and power. He tore up Lake County in the first half of 2019, finally flashing the power and speed combo that was so tantalizing at draft time. Unfortunately, Benson struggled after a promotion and failed to maintain his breakout. Just 21 years old, the end isn't in sight for Benson. Yet, he will need to curb his strikeout issues if he's to avoid the wrong side of a different sword—that of Damocles.

YEAR	TEAM	LVL	AGE	PA	DRC+	VORP	BABIP	BRR	FRAA	WARP
2017	MHV	A-	19	236	108	11.6	.339	0.1	RF(56): -2.5	0.3
2018	LKC	A	20	506	89	5.6	.218	-0.4	RF(113): 5.4, CF(4): -0.2	0.9
2019	LKC	A	21	259	140	25.6	.325	1.5	RF(21): -0.8, LF(20): 0.7	1.6
2019	LYN	A+	21	255	79	1.3	.255	3.5	LF(37): -3.0, RF(15): -1.1	-0.1
2020	CLE	MLB	22	251	54	-6.9	.264	0.2	RF -1, LF 0	-0.8

Aaron Bracho 2B

Born: 04/24/01   Age: 19   Bats: B   Throws: R
Height: 5'11"   Weight: 175   Origin: International Free Agent, 2017

YEAR	TEAM	LVL	AGE	PA	R	2B	3B	HR	RBI	BB	K	SB	CS	AVG/OBP/SLG
2019	CLT	RK	18	137	25	10	2	6	29	23	21	4	1	.296/.416/.593
2019	MHV	A-	18	32	5	1	0	2	4	5	8	0	0	.222/.344/.481
2020	CLE	MLB	19	251	25	12	1	5	25	30	69	3	1	.210/.310/.346

Comparables: Joey Gallo, Daniel Robertson, Logan Morrison

When Cleveland landed Bracho for $1.5 million in July 2017, they saw an infielder who had a good idea at the plate and could even add a little pop. And that's pretty much exactly what the 18-year-old switch hitter has been, recording Votto-like walk rates in two stops in 2019, culminating with a late-season cup of coffee in Mahoning Valley. There's still some swing-and-miss in his game, but it's not too hard to envision a 20-25 homer profile with a glove that permits him to play up-the-middle.

YEAR	TEAM	LVL	AGE	PA	DRC+	VORP	BABIP	BRR	FRAA	WARP
2019	CLT	RK	18	137	186	22.8	.306	0.9	2B(22): 1.0	1.5
2019	MHV	A-	18	32	93	2.3	.235	0.3	2B(8): -1.4	0.0
2020	CLE	MLB	19	251	81	2.1	.281	0.0	2B 0	0.2

Bobby Bradley 1B

Born: 05/29/96   Age: 24   Bats: L   Throws: R
Height: 6'1"   Weight: 225   Origin: Round 3, 2014 Draft (#97 overall)

YEAR	TEAM	LVL	AGE	PA	R	2B	3B	HR	RBI	BB	K	SB	CS	AVG/OBP/SLG
2017	AKR	AA	21	532	66	25	3	23	89	55	122	3	3	.251/.331/.465
2018	AKR	AA	22	421	49	19	3	24	64	45	105	1	0	.214/.304/.477
2018	COH	AAA	22	128	11	7	2	3	19	11	43	0	0	.254/.323/.430
2019	COH	AAA	23	453	65	23	0	33	74	46	153	0	0	.264/.344/.567
2019	CLE	MLB	23	49	4	5	0	1	4	4	20	0	0	.178/.245/.356
2020	CLE	MLB	24	105	11	5	0	4	13	8	39	0	0	.200/.271/.385

Comparables: Dick Gernert, Tyler O'Neill, Ryan McMahon

In the last two seasons, Bradley has been referred to as bulky, a large adult son and the usher of BIG BOY SZN in Cleveland. It's hard to argue with much of that, but there's not a whole lot else to say. Bradley's skill set is a little like putting a Charger engine in a go-kart: there's power, for sure, but it's mostly wasted. In a 15-game cameo with the big club this season, Bradley forgot to bring two of the Three True Outcomes—the "good" two, as it were. He struck out in over 40 percent of his trips to the dish while managing all of one home run. There's obviously still time for Bradley to shape himself into a productive big-league hitter—he did smack 33 homers in Triple-A, after all—but his contact woes are a legitimate threat to him becoming more than a Quad-A type.

YEAR	TEAM	LVL	AGE	PA	DRC+	VORP	BABIP	BRR	FRAA	WARP
2017	AKR	AA	21	532	120	17.4	.287	-2.6	1B(125): -6.3	0.9
2018	AKR	AA	22	421	109	17.0	.226	-2.3	1B(97): 1.4	0.8
2018	COH	AAA	22	128	101	2.8	.377	0.3	1B(29): 1.5	0.3
2019	COH	AAA	23	453	124	16.7	.336	-2.5	1B(97): 1.9	1.7
2019	CLE	MLB	23	49	54	-2.2	.292	-0.1	1B(5): -0.2	-0.2
2020	CLE	MLB	24	105	72	-2.4	.285	-0.2	1B 0	-0.3

Tyler Freeman SS

Born: 05/21/99   Age: 21   Bats: R   Throws: R
Height: 6'0"   Weight: 170   Origin: Round 2, 2017 Draft (#71 overall)

YEAR	TEAM	LVL	AGE	PA	R	2B	3B	HR	RBI	BB	K	SB	CS	AVG/OBP/SLG
2017	CLE	RK	18	144	19	9	0	2	14	7	12	5	1	.297/.364/.414
2018	MHV	A-	19	301	49	29	4	2	38	8	22	14	3	.352/.405/.511
2019	LKC	A	20	272	51	16	3	3	24	18	28	11	4	.292/.382/.424
2019	LYN	A+	20	275	38	16	2	0	20	8	25	8	1	.319/.354/.397
2020	CLE	MLB	21	251	24	14	1	3	24	14	35	4	1	.267/.331/.380

Comparables: Isiah Kiner-Falefa, Thairo Estrada, José Altuve

Freeman's ability to make contact is such that he's a legitimate prospect despite not doing much else at the dish. He posted the second-highest average in the Carolina League as a 20-year-old, which is something, and he did so while playing passable defense at the six. It's not your typical profile, and there's obviously a good deal of downside in the profile—his hit tool has to play well-above-average to give him a chance to start—but it's working for now and that's the best any of us can aspire to.

YEAR	TEAM	LVL	AGE	PA	DRC+	VORP	BABIP	BRR	FRAA	WARP
2017	CLE	RK	18	144	117	12.9	.313	1.8	SS(29): -0.1, 2B(4): -0.9	0.9
2018	MHV	A-	19	301	189	37.7	.372	3.5	SS(52): -0.1, 2B(10): -0.2	3.7
2019	LKC	A	20	272	142	25.1	.320	2.6	SS(57): 0.5, 2B(3): -0.2	2.6
2019	LYN	A+	20	275	129	16.7	.350	1.2	SS(56): -1.0, 2B(3): 0.1	1.9
2020	CLE	MLB	21	251	91	5.3	.304	0.0	SS 1, 2B 0	0.6

Daniel Johnson OF

Born: 07/11/95   Age: 24   Bats: L   Throws: L
Height: 5'10"   Weight: 200   Origin: Round 5, 2016 Draft (#154 overall)

YEAR	TEAM	LVL	AGE	PA	R	2B	3B	HR	RBI	BB	K	SB	CS	AVG/OBP/SLG
2017	HAG	A	21	364	61	16	4	17	52	22	70	12	9	.300/.361/.529
2017	POT	A+	21	185	22	13	0	5	20	13	30	10	2	.294/.346/.459
2018	HAR	AA	22	391	48	19	7	6	31	23	90	21	4	.267/.321/.410
2019	AKR	AA	23	167	25	7	2	10	33	16	39	6	3	.253/.337/.534
2019	COH	AAA	23	380	51	27	5	9	44	34	79	6	7	.306/.371/.496
2020	CLE	MLB	24	105	11	5	1	4	13	7	27	3	1	.245/.305/.425

Comparables: Zoilo Almonte, Cedric Mullins, Austin Hays

It was a good year for Johnson, who was traded from the Nationals to Cleveland as part of the Yan Gomes swap. How good? He played in the second-most games of his career, and posted a new career-high OPS. There are some hit-tool concerns here, and not all of his power followed him to his stint in Columbus. But he has a big-time arm and louder tools than he's shown for most of his minor-league career. Johnson should receive a big-league opportunity in 2020, and in time could look like a savvy pick-up.

YEAR	TEAM	LVL	AGE	PA	DRC+	VORP	BABIP	BRR	FRAA	WARP
2017	HAG	A	21	364	142	30.7	.333	-0.5	RF(51): -1.1, CF(15): 0.3	2.3
2017	POT	A+	21	185	119	10.2	.331	1.7	CF(30): -3.2, RF(9): 3.5	1.1
2018	HAR	AA	22	391	96	7.6	.338	-2.3	RF(54): 6.3, CF(33): -2.9	0.9
2019	AKR	AA	23	167	122	12.0	.276	-2.3	CF(24): -2.3, RF(10): -0.3	0.2
2019	COH	AAA	23	380	123	18.0	.370	-1.5	RF(47): 6.4, CF(21): 1.2	2.4
2020	CLE	MLB	24	105	92	2.2	.304	-0.1	CF -1, RF 0	0.2

Nolan Jones 3B

Born: 05/07/98   Age: 22   Bats: L   Throws: R
Height: 6'2"   Weight: 185   Origin: Round 2, 2016 Draft (#55 overall)

YEAR	TEAM	LVL	AGE	PA	R	2B	3B	HR	RBI	BB	K	SB	CS	AVG/OBP/SLG
2017	MHV	A-	19	265	41	18	3	4	33	43	60	1	0	.317/.430/.482
2018	LKC	A	20	389	46	12	0	16	49	63	97	2	1	.279/.393/.464
2018	LYN	A+	20	130	23	9	0	3	17	26	34	0	0	.298/.438/.471
2019	LYN	A+	21	324	48	12	1	7	41	65	85	5	3	.286/.435/.425
2019	AKR	AA	21	211	33	10	2	8	22	31	63	2	0	.253/.370/.466
2020	CLE	MLB	22	251	28	12	1	8	29	29	85	0	0	.240/.333/.405

Comparables: Drew Robinson, Lewis Brinson, Shed Long

An appropriate response to Jones's minor-league career is that Larry David GIF. You know the one. On one hand, Jones has incrementally tapped into his raw power over the last couple seasons, a skill that pairs beautifully with his plus plate discipline. On the other, he struck out almost a third of the time at Double-A this season, which is too frequently to feel good about. It doesn't help that Jones's defense is nearly as polarizing. He has more than enough arm for the hot corner, yet his actions there are likely to cap his ceiling around "tolerable." Back and forth, back and forth. Jones is a solid prospect, but he's also a liquid one.

YEAR	TEAM	LVL	AGE	PA	DRC+	VORP	BABIP	BRR	FRAA	WARP
2017	MHV	A-	19	265	182	28.6	.417	1.7	3B(53): 0.0	2.8
2018	LKC	A	20	389	155	33.5	.347	-0.9	3B(77): -4.1	2.9
2018	LYN	A+	20	130	159	12.7	.418	0.1	3B(28): -0.3	1.1
2019	LYN	A+	21	324	172	28.7	.399	-1.4	3B(72): -3.4	2.8
2019	AKR	AA	21	211	150	17.0	.346	0.8	3B(43): 0.0	1.8
2020	CLE	MLB	22	251	97	6.8	.352	-0.3	3B -1	0.6

Bo Naylor   C

Born: 02/21/00   Age: 20   Bats: L   Throws: R
Height: 6'0"   Weight: 195   Origin: Round 1, 2018 Draft (#29 overall)

YEAR	TEAM	LVL	AGE	PA	R	2B	3B	HR	RBI	BB	K	SB	CS	AVG/OBP/SLG
2018	CLT	RK	18	139	17	3	3	2	17	21	28	5	1	.274/.381/.402
2019	LKC	A	19	453	60	18	10	11	65	43	104	7	5	.243/.313/.421
2020	CLE	MLB	20	251	23	11	2	6	26	22	72	1	0	.216/.289/.359

Comparables: Rio Ruiz, Kyle Skipworth, Joe Benson

A year after being selected in the first round, Naylor has assuaged initial concerns about his likelihood of sticking behind the plate. There are still some questions about his arm strength, but quick hands and athleticism have righted a lot of wrongs so far. Offensively, Naylor gave back some of his usefulness with both average and walk rate, yet the uptick in power production was encouraging. He's still years away from factoring into Cleveland's big-league plans. But there's plenty to like here.

YEAR	TEAM	LVL	AGE	PA	DRC+	VORP	BABIP	BRR	FRAA	WARP
2018	CLT	RK	18	139	124	12.2	.341	0.3	C(19): -0.4, 3B(5): -0.7	0.7
2019	LKC	A	19	453	98	20.9	.296	0.9	C(85): 3.4	2.2
2020	CLE	MLB	20	251	74	-0.5	.290	-0.1	C 0, 3B 0	0.0

Brayan Rocchio SS

Born: 01/13/01   Age: 19   Bats: B   Throws: R
Height: 5'10"   Weight: 150   Origin: International Free Agent, 2017

YEAR	TEAM	LVL	AGE	PA	R	2B	3B	HR	RBI	BB	K	SB	CS	AVG/OBP/SLG
2018	DIN	RK	17	111	19	2	3	1	12	5	14	8	5	.323/.391/.434
2018	CLT	RK	17	158	21	10	1	1	17	10	17	14	8	.343/.389/.448
2019	MHV	A-	18	295	33	12	3	5	27	20	40	14	8	.250/.310/.373
2020	CLE	MLB	19	251	24	11	1	5	25	17	53	9	5	.242/.301/.367

Comparables: Enrique Hernández, Amed Rosario, Juniel Querecuto

Rocchio was born just five months before the release of *The Fast and the Furious*, which is astounding because there's a decent chance those films continue to be made into his retirement—and that isn't a knock on his career prospects. A nitrous oxide boost for Rocchio's bat would be nice, as the Venezuelan's lumber is a little light on the pop, but even if the power doesn't come, he'll still be a top-flight defender with plus hit and run tools. It's definitely a profile worthy of a Corona at the family barbecue, or a public spat between Dwayne "The Rock" Johnson and Tyrese.

YEAR	TEAM	LVL	AGE	PA	DRC+	VORP	BABIP	BRR	FRAA	WARP
2018	DIN	RK	17	111	136	9.7	.369	-1.0	SS(15): -0.2, 2B(8): 0.6	0.8
2018	CLT	RK	17	158	161	15.0	.378	1.2	SS(26): 5.2, 3B(8): -1.1	2.0
2019	MHV	A-	18	295	107	12.8	.276	-1.8	SS(62): 5.5, 2B(6): 0.6	1.8
2020	CLE	MLB	19	251	79	1.1	.293	-0.1	SS 2, 2B 0	0.3

Ka'ai Tom OF

Born: 05/29/94   Age: 26   Bats: L   Throws: R
Height: 5'9"   Weight: 190   Origin: Round 5, 2015 Draft (#154 overall)

YEAR	TEAM	LVL	AGE	PA	R	2B	3B	HR	RBI	BB	K	SB	CS	AVG/OBP/SLG
2017	LYN	A+	23	529	68	31	7	10	65	59	100	23	6	.254/.340/.418
2018	AKR	AA	24	484	60	21	4	12	64	46	102	13	10	.245/.329/.399
2019	AKR	AA	25	343	50	12	6	14	42	43	73	3	2	.285/.386/.512
2019	COH	AAA	25	211	33	15	4	9	44	21	53	2	3	.298/.370/.564
2020	CLE	MLB	26	251	29	12	2	10	33	23	68	5	2	.245/.322/.444

Comparables: Andy Parrino, Melky Mesa, Skye Bolt

Here's a cool story about Tom. He was born in Hawaii and played both baseball and football in high school. It was on the gridiron that he was teammates with former Heisman Trophy winner Marcus Mariota. Another cool story about Tom: Ka'ai is his middle name and his given name is actually Blaze. One more cool story about Tom: he tore through two minor-league levels last season, smacking more homers than all but three other Cleveland minor leaguers while playing strong center-field defense. Provided he can keep his swing-and-miss in check, he's likely to debut in 2020.

YEAR	TEAM	LVL	AGE	PA	DRC+	VORP	BABIP	BRR	FRAA	WARP
2017	LYN	A+	23	529	120	31.8	.299	2.8	CF(47): -1.8, RF(35): -0.2	2.6
2018	AKR	AA	24	484	108	26.3	.291	-0.3	CF(54): -1.4, RF(35): 9.5	2.7
2019	AKR	AA	25	343	149	31.7	.335	2.2	RF(32): -3.0, CF(31): -6.2	1.7
2019	COH	AAA	25	211	131	14.6	.370	0.7	LF(19): -0.6, RF(16): 0.5	1.4
2020	CLE	MLB	26	251	102	8.7	.309	0.0	CF -1, RF 0	0.9

George Valera   OF

Born: 11/13/00   Age: 19   Bats: L   Throws: L
Height: 5'10"   Weight: 160   Origin: International Free Agent, 2017

YEAR	TEAM	LVL	AGE	PA	R	2B	3B	HR	RBI	BB	K	SB	CS	AVG/OBP/SLG
2019	MHV	A-	18	188	22	7	1	8	29	29	52	6	2	.236/.356/.446
2019	LKC	A	18	26	1	0	1	0	3	2	9	0	2	.087/.192/.174
2020	CLE	MLB	19	251	24	11	1	7	26	22	85	3	2	.202/.278/.344

Comparables: Ronald Acuña Jr., Carson Kelly, Victor Robles

You know the adage, about how development isn't linear? Good, because Valera is evidence of that. His 2019 statistics were—to be charitable—not what you want. It mostly doesn't matter though because of his physical traits. Scouts rave about his projectible hit tool and his chances of posting a .300 average with 25 or so home runs at maturity. Oftentimes potential is never realized, or is lost to the heavens through injury or other reasons beyond our understanding—call it the angel's share if you'd like. But it's too early to say that will be the case here. As such, keep an eye on Valera—just not while driving.

YEAR	TEAM	LVL	AGE	PA	DRC+	VORP	BABIP	BRR	FRAA	WARP
2019	MHV	A-	18	188	132	11.8	.296	-0.3	CF(25): 0.7, RF(11): -3.5	1.1
2019	LKC	A	18	26	35	-3.4	.143	-1.0	RF(3): 1.2, LF(2): 1.6	0.0
2020	CLE	MLB	19	251	68	-2.7	.290	-0.5	CF -1, RF -1	-0.5

Bradley Zimmer CF

Born: 11/27/92 Age: 27 Bats: L Throws: R
Height: 6'5" Weight: 220 Origin: Round 1, 2014 Draft (#21 overall)

YEAR	TEAM	LVL	AGE	PA	R	2B	3B	HR	RBI	BB	K	SB	CS	AVG/OBP/SLG
2017	COH	AAA	24	144	22	11	2	5	14	14	43	9	3	.294/.371/.532
2017	CLE	MLB	24	332	41	15	2	8	39	26	99	18	1	.241/.307/.385
2018	COH	AAA	25	28	1	0	0	1	1	1	11	1	0	.148/.179/.259
2018	CLE	MLB	25	114	14	5	0	2	9	7	44	4	1	.226/.281/.330
2019	COH	AAA	26	26	5	1	1	1	2	3	6	2	0	.364/.440/.636
2019	CLE	MLB	26	14	1	0	0	0	0	1	7	0	0	.000/.071/.000
2020	CLE	MLB	27	105	11	4	0	3	12	9	35	5	1	.219/.303/.373

Comparables: Jordan Danks, Kirk Nieuwenhuis, Dexter Fowler

Zimmer's injury woes the past few seasons would not fit comfortably within the allotted run time of a "House" episode. He wedged his way into Cleveland's long-term plans with a pretty good, if not awe-inspiring, rookie campaign, before having since succumbed to several maulings by the injury bug. There was a bruised rib, then shoulder surgery, then recovery from shoulder surgery. He's appeared in just 43 games over the past two years as a result, and hasn't rapped a hit since June 2018—even Vanilla Ice is like, c'mon, buddy. The tools for Zimmer are still there, it's really all about the durability.

YEAR	TEAM	LVL	AGE	PA	DRC+	VORP	BABIP	BRR	FRAA	WARP
2017	COH	AAA	24	144	129	9.9	.405	-0.6	CF(26): 3.6, RF(8): 0.5	1.2
2017	CLE	MLB	24	332	70	7.3	.328	1.6	CF(97): 9.5	1.0
2018	COH	AAA	25	28	8	-2.4	.200	0.1	CF(5): -0.2	-0.2
2018	CLE	MLB	25	114	49	-0.7	.367	1.4	CF(34): 5.4	0.4
2019	COH	AAA	26	26	112	4.5	.467	0.6	CF(6): -0.1	0.2
2019	CLE	MLB	26	14	71	-0.1	.000	0.3	RF(4): -0.4, CF(2): 0.2	0.0
2020	CLE	MLB	27	105	83	1.2	.314	0.2	CF 2, RF 0	0.3

Daniel Espino RHP

Born: 01/05/01   Age: 19   Bats: R   Throws: R
Height: 6'2"   Weight: 205   Origin: Round 1, 2019 Draft (#24 overall)

YEAR	TEAM	LVL	AGE	W	L	SV	G	GS	IP	H	HR	BB/9	K/9	K	GB%	BABIP
2019	CLE	RK	18	0	1	0	6	6	13²	7	1	3.3	10.5	16	50%	.207
2019	MHV	A-	18	0	2	0	3	3	10	9	1	4.5	16.2	18	32%	.381
2020	CLE	MLB	19	2	2	0	33	0	35	36	6	3.7	9.3	36	38%	.311

Comparables: Pedro Avila, Jake Thompson, Jenrry Mejia

Espino was Cleveland's first pick in June's draft and the proud recipient of a $2.5 million signing bonus (enough shells to convince him he didn't really want to have to find his way around LSU's campus). He's on the smaller side, but makes up for it with extreme flexibility and arm speed. In the past, Espino has touched triple digits with his heater. In the future, he might pair the fastball with two high-quality secondary offerings. Expect the slow-and-low treatment, but Espino is otherwise one to know.

YEAR	TEAM	LVL	AGE	WHIP	ERA	DRA	WARP	MPH	FB%	WHF	CSP
2019	CLE	RK	18	0.88	1.98	1.65	0.6				
2019	MHV	A-	18	1.40	6.30	2.96	0.3				
2020	CLE	MLB	19	1.43	4.75	4.93	0.1				

Ethan Hankins   RHP

Born: 05/23/00   Age: 20   Bats: R   Throws: R
Height: 6'6"   Weight: 200   Origin: Round 1C, 2018 Draft (#35 overall)

YEAR	TEAM	LVL	AGE	W	L	SV	G	GS	IP	H	HR	BB/9	K/9	K	GB%	BABIP
2019	MHV	A-	19	0	0	0	9	8	38²	23	1	4.2	10.0	43	61%	.232
2019	LKC	A	19	0	3	0	5	5	21¹	20	3	5.1	11.8	28	49%	.340
2020	CLE	MLB	20	2	2	0	33	0	35	35	6	3.7	8.4	33	49%	.297

Comparables: Pedro Avila, Joe Ross, Jake Thompson

Bringing along a starting pitching prospect is a little like teaching a kid how to ride a bike: the main goal is to prevent injury. Hankins was a candidate for the top spot in the 2018 draft before a shoulder injury cost him a couple ticks of velocity and his chance at going first overall. Cleveland scooped him up later in the first round and has kept on his training wheels thus far, permitting him to just 63 innings in his first season two seasons as a pro. Hankins exceeded five innings of work just once in 2019, but gaudy strikeout numbers bode well for his future prospects as a potential top-end starter (though not his, well, gaudy walk totals). With linear progression, next season should see him pedaling furiously with GM Mike Chernoff running beside the bike and steadying the back of his seat before finally letting go. In baseball terms, that means we should get to see Hankins pump a high-90s heater while also baffling hitters with a pair of strong secondaries.

YEAR	TEAM	LVL	AGE	WHIP	ERA	DRA	WARP	MPH	FB%	WHF	CSP
2019	MHV	A-	19	1.06	1.40	3.30	0.8				
2019	LKC	A	19	1.50	4.64	5.49	-0.1				
2020	CLE	MLB	20	1.41	4.67	4.87	0.1				

James Karinchak   RHP

Born: 09/22/95   Age: 24   Bats: R   Throws: R
Height: 6'3"   Weight: 230   Origin: Round 9, 2017 Draft (#282 overall)

YEAR	TEAM	LVL	AGE	W	L	SV	G	GS	IP	H	HR	BB/9	K/9	K	GB%	BABIP
2017	MHV	A-	21	2	2	0	10	6	23^1	30	1	3.5	12.0	31	30%	.468
2018	LKC	A	22	3	0	1	7	0	11^1	8	0	5.6	15.9	20	55%	.400
2018	LYN	A+	22	1	1	13	25	0	27	14	1	5.7	15.0	45	40%	.295
2018	AKR	AA	22	0	1	0	10	0	10^1	7	1	10.5	13.9	16	29%	.300
2019	AKR	AA	23	0	0	6	10	0	10	2	0	1.8	21.6	24	56%	.222
2019	COH	AAA	23	1	1	2	17	0	17^1	14	2	6.8	21.8	42	48%	.571
2019	CLE	MLB	23	0	0	0	5	0	5^1	3	0	1.7	13.5	8	38%	.231
2020	*CLE*	*MLB*	*24*	*2*	*2*	*0*	*45*	*0*	*48*	*42*	*7*	*4.5*	*8.3*	*44*	*42%*	*.270*

Comparables: Jensen Lewis, Rogelio Armenteros, Aaron Blair

In 1998, Irvine Welsh wrote *Filth*, a crime novel that was later turned into a film starring James McAvoy. The book was about a hallucinating misanthrope who solved crimes. The title, however, would be apt for a book (probably a novella) about Karinchak's curveball—an offering who has already been featured plenty on the smallest screen via Pitching Ninja's acclaimed Twitter account. He used the curveball to great success in 2019, punching out 74 guys in just over 30 innings of minor-league work and earning a late-season promotion to the majors. His strikeout numbers weren't as prodigious in Cleveland, albeit in a small sample, but they were still super good. Something that bodes well for him should it continue: his 16 percent swinging-strike rate would have placed him among the league's best.

YEAR	TEAM	LVL	AGE	WHIP	ERA	DRA	WARP	MPH	FB%	WHF	CSP
2017	MHV	A-	21	1.67	5.79	7.07	-0.5				
2018	LKC	A	22	1.32	0.79	3.41	0.2				
2018	LYN	A+	22	1.15	1.00	2.77	0.7				
2018	AKR	AA	22	1.84	2.61	5.59	-0.1				
2019	AKR	AA	23	0.40	0.00	1.80	0.3				
2019	COH	AAA	23	1.56	4.67	2.12	0.7				
2019	CLE	MLB	23	0.75	1.69	3.89	0.1	97.7	56.4	18.1	47.8
2020	*CLE*	*MLB*	*24*	*1.38*	*4.08*	*4.27*	*0.5*	*97.5*	*58.1*	*18.6*	*49.2*

Triston McKenzie RHP

Born: 08/02/97   Age: 22   Bats: R   Throws: R
Height: 6'5"   Weight: 165   Origin: Round 1, 2015 Draft (#42 overall)

YEAR	TEAM	LVL	AGE	W	L	SV	G	GS	IP	H	HR	BB/9	K/9	K	GB%	BABIP
2017	LYN	A+	19	12	6	0	25	25	143	105	14	2.8	11.7	186	43%	.283
2018	AKR	AA	20	7	4	0	16	16	90²	63	8	2.8	8.6	87	34%	.234
2020	CLE	MLB	22	2	2	0	33	0	35	35	6	3.2	8.9	35	36%	.303

Comparables: Adrian Morejon, Chris Tillman, Arodys Vizcaíno

Everything is skinny these days—jeans, margaritas, even pitchers. McKenzie is charitably listed at 165 pounds despite a 6-foot-5 frame. His lithe nature has caused concerns in the past about his viability as a starter—scouts tend to like to see pitchers with broad shoulders and developed frames, believing those pitchers are better equipped to handle a rigorous workload. Those worries aren't going anyway anytime soon. He was shut down with a back injury in early March, and never returned to make a start, giving him two consecutive injury-plagued years. He's still just 22, so there's plenty of book left to be written. But another thin year will leave him with slim chances of remaining a starter.

YEAR	TEAM	LVL	AGE	WHIP	ERA	DRA	WARP	MPH	FB%	WHF	CSP
2017	LYN	A+	19	1.05	3.46	3.21	3.5				
2018	AKR	AA	20	1.00	2.68	3.05	2.4				
2020	CLE	MLB	22	1.37	4.51	4.72	0.2				

Danny Salazar   RHP

Born: 01/11/90   Age: 30   Bats: R   Throws: R
Height: 6'0"   Weight: 195   Origin: International Free Agent, 2006

YEAR	TEAM	LVL	AGE	W	L	SV	G	GS	IP	H	HR	BB/9	K/9	K	GB%	BABIP
2017	COH	AAA	27	1	1	0	2	2	9¹	6	3	4.8	12.5	13	37%	.188
2017	CLE	MLB	27	5	6	0	23	19	103	94	14	3.8	12.7	145	39%	.343
2019	AKR	AA	29	0	1	0	5	4	8¹	8	1	6.5	7.6	7	58%	.280
2019	COH	AAA	29	0	0	0	2	2	7¹	4	0	2.5	13.5	11	40%	.267
2019	CLE	MLB	29	0	1	0	1	1	4	4	2	6.8	4.5	2	42%	.200
2020	CLE	MLB	30	1	2	0	33	0	35	42	16	4.4	8.1	32	37%	.270

Comparables: Chris Archer, Rogelio Armenteros, Sonny Gray

Six years ago, the world was a vastly different place. Apple's earbuds had cords; reality TV game-show hosts stuck to reality TV game shows; and Mike Trout was getting robbed of MVP Awards (okay, maybe not *everything* has changed). Salazar, then a 23-year-old rookie, was chucking gas, punching out almost 31 percent of batters faced and starting the Wild Card Game. He was, in so many words, establishing himself as one of the most exciting young starters in the game. Now 29 years old, Salazar's body has failed him. He's thrown four innings the last two seasons, and he sat in the mid-80s in his most recent outing. Afterward, he requested time off to consider his career. If this is it for Salazar, it went by quickly—too quickly—but boy, oh boy, was he fun.

YEAR	TEAM	LVL	AGE	WHIP	ERA	DRA	WARP	MPH	FB%	WHF	CSP
2017	COH	AAA	27	1.18	2.89	3.79	0.2				
2017	CLE	MLB	27	1.34	4.28	3.54	2.3	97.5	59.7	17.3	45.8
2019	AKR	AA	29	1.68	5.40	6.07	-0.1				
2019	COH	AAA	29	0.82	0.00	2.14	0.3				
2019	CLE	MLB	29	1.75	4.50	7.32	-0.1	88.5	31.8	4.5	38.4
2020	CLE	MLB	30	1.68	8.22	6.87	-0.6	96.2	57.9	16.6	41.1

LINEOUTS

Hitters

HITTER	POS	TEAM	LVL	AGE	PA	R	2B	3B	HR	RBI	BB	K	SB	CS	AVG/OBP/SLG	DRC+	WARP
Christian Arroyo	3B	DUR	AAA	24	134	21	9	1	8	29	12	26	1	0	.314/.381/.603	144	1.3
	3B	TBA	MLB	24	57	8	2	0	2	7	5	18	0	0	.220/.304/.380	73	0.0
Christian Cairo	SS	CLE	Rk	18	179	26	3	1	0	9	25	40	7	3	.178/.324/.212	75	0.3
Ernie Clement	SS	AKR	AA	23	437	46	15	3	1	24	26	33	16	10	.261/.314/.322	116	3.5
Joseph Naranjo	1B	CLE	Rk	18	200	25	5	2	1	21	22	44	1	0	.266/.345/.333	102	0.5
Hanley Ramirez	SS	CLE	MLB	35	57	4	1	0	2	8	8	17	0	0	.184/.298/.327	79	0.0
Gabriel Rodriguez	SS	CLE	Rk	17	73	7	3	0	0	10	4	22	1	1	.215/.288/.262	40	-0.3
Yordys Valdes	SS	CLE	Rk	17	181	17	3	1	2	11	16	53	15	4	.179/.251/.247	34	-0.3
Andrew Velazquez	UT	COH	AAA	24	46	5	4	1	0	5	0	9	1	1	.244/.261/.378	79	-0.3
	UT	DUR	AAA	24	141	20	9	1	4	16	10	30	2	4	.271/.329/.450	75	0.1
	UT	CLE	MLB	24	12	1	1	0	0	0	1	7	1	0	.091/.167/.182	25	-0.1
	UT	TBA	MLB	24	12	2	1	0	0	0	0	6	0	0	.083/.083/.167	67	-0.1

Christian Arroyo spent time near bays on both coasts before finding himself dumped on Cleveland at the deadline. He struggled at the plate before a barking elbow shut him down for good in June. ⊗ The Indians gave 2019 fourth rounder **Christian Cairo** more than twice his slot value to lure him away from a scholarship at LSU, proving once again that the "stay in school" messaging works only when the alternative isn't a boatload of cash. ⊗ **Ernie Clement**, who struck out a measly seven times his junior year, could be bringing his high-contact bat and flexible glove to Cleveland in short order. ⊗ A Google search for **Luis Durango Jr.** returns hits mostly concerning his father, who played in the majors for two different organizations. The magic number for bragging rights is 40 games. ⊗ Cleveland went overslot to coax **Joseph Naranjo** away from Cal State Fullerton, betting on a little extra pop from an otherwise James Loney-esque first-base prospect. ⊗ It was a long short year for **Hanley Ramirez**. He scored Cleveland's first run of the season with a homer, but limped (both figuratively and literally) to a sub-Mendoza line average before receiving a late-April release. This might be the end. ⊗ Cleveland clearly followed their own instructions for finding toolsy, flexible middle infielders when they signed **Gabriel Rodriguez** for a cool $2.1 million in July 2018. The 17-year-old flashed a little pop and a little speed, but will require a lot more time in the oven. ⊗ **Yordys Valdes** spurned Florida State with Tebow-like precision when he traded in his commitment to join Cleveland for a cool mil. Valdes then hit .179/.251/.247 with Tebow-like precision in his first taste of pro ball. ⊗ Though **Andrew Velazquez** is from the Bronx, he hasn't been a bomber during his big-league career—not in a good way, at least. His positional flexibility could come in handy off the bench, but he needs to make more contact.

Pitchers

PITCHER	TEAM	LVL	AGE	W	L	SV	G	GS	IP	H	HR	BB/9	K/9	K	GB%	WHIP	ERA	DRA	WARP
Cody Anderson	COH	AAA	28	0	2	0	6	6	23²	25	3	2.7	8.0	21	54%	1.35	4.56	5.05	0.4
	CLE	MLB	28	0	1	0	5	2	8²	12	1	8.3	9.3	9	29%	2.31	9.35	7.60	-0.2
Jon Edwards	COH	AAA	31	6	1	3	41	0	49	43	7	4.8	11.4	62	40%	1.41	4.22	3.70	1.2
	CLE	MLB	31	2	0	0	9	0	8	5	2	6.8	5.6	5	44%	1.38	2.25	9.19	-0.3
Sam Hentges	AKR	AA	22	2	13	0	26	26	128²	148	11	4.5	8.8	126	36%	1.65	5.11	7.13	-3.4
James Hoyt	COH	AAA	32	2	0	4	40	2	42	46	3	4.3	10.3	48	53%	1.57	3.43	5.02	0.5
	CLE	MLB	32	0	0	0	8	0	8¹	6	2	2.2	10.8	10	45%	0.96	2.16	5.12	0.0
Phil Maton	ELP	AAA	26	2	1	2	13	0	18²	17	2	2.9	14.5	30	59%	1.23	2.89	1.80	0.8
	COH	AAA	26	0	1	3	9	0	10²	5	1	3.4	14.3	17	44%	0.84	2.53	1.91	0.4
	CLE	MLB	26	0	0	0	9	0	12¹	4	1	4.4	9.5	13	46%	0.81	2.92	2.67	0.4
	SDN	MLB	26	0	0	0	21	0	24¹	34	6	2.2	7.4	20	47%	1.64	7.77	5.69	-0.1
Jean Carlos Mejia	LYN	A+	22	3	1	0	8	8	33	28	0	2.5	9.8	36	57%	1.12	4.09	3.76	0.5
Elijah Morgan	LYN	A+	23	3	1	0	6	6	33²	19	3	1.3	10.7	40	25%	0.71	1.87	2.43	1.1
	AKR	AA	23	6	4	0	19	18	102	100	12	2.9	9.2	104	33%	1.30	3.79	5.23	-0.4
Scott Moss	CHT	AA	24	6	5	0	20	20	102	84	7	5.0	10.9	123	39%	1.38	3.44	4.51	0.6
	AKR	AA	24	2	0	0	2	2	10	3	0	4.5	11.7	13	35%	0.80	0.00	2.83	0.3
	COH	AAA	24	2	1	0	4	4	18²	12	1	3.9	11.1	23	29%	1.07	1.93	2.41	0.8
Dan Otero	COH	AAA	34	0	0	0	11	0	12¹	5	1	0.7	5.8	8	74%	0.49	0.73	1.70	0.5
	CLE	MLB	34	0	0	0	25	0	29²	42	6	0.9	4.9	16	53%	1.52	4.85	7.09	-0.6
Luis Oviedo	LKC	A	20	6	6	0	19	19	87	80	6	4.1	7.4	72	43%	1.38	5.38	4.98	0.2
Adam Plutko	COH	AAA	27	1	3	0	4	4	15²	21	1	2.3	9.2	16	22%	1.60	7.47	6.59	0.0
	CLE	MLB	27	7	5	0	21	20	109¹	115	22	2.1	6.4	78	32%	1.29	4.86	7.76	-2.4
Nick Sandlin	AKR	AA	22	0	0	2	15	0	17¹	13	2	4.2	14.0	27	49%	1.21	1.56	4.22	0.1
	COH	AAA	22	1	0	0	9	0	9	5	2	7.0	11.0	11	53%	1.33	4.00	3.56	0.2
Carlos Vargas	MHV	A-	19	6	4	0	15	15	77²	73	4	2.8	8.2	71	48%	1.25	4.52	4.82	0.3

It was a tough acronym year for **Cody Anderson**. After missing most of the last two seasons due to TJS, he returned to the bigs and posted ugly ERA and DRA before requiring another trip to the IL. His next acronym will be "AAA" or "DFA." ⓘ If you need someone to take your dog for a stroll around the block, you might want to consider **Jon Edwards** for the job. Because he's good at walks, you see. Unfortunately, that's not a great trait for a professional pitcher. ⓘ **Sam Hentges** is a 6-foot-8 lefty who pumps 95 mph fastballs. That's great. He also walked nearly five dudes per nine innings in Double-A, which, uh, is not. ⓘ **James Hoyt** has at times over the years looked like a legit relief option, pairing a mid-90s sinker with a wipeout slider that gets an obscene number of swinging strikes. He turned 33 in September, so we're getting near now-or-never territory. ⊗ The Maton family has produced three MLB draftees. **Phil Maton**, the elder of the trio, has more than 120 big-league innings to his name. He has an uptempo delivery and a high-spin fastball, but there's a chance he ends up the Cooper Manning of the bunch. ⊗ **Juan Carlos Mejía** was on the rise thanks to his mid-90s sinker and high groundball rate. His season ended after eight starts due to hernia surgery, delaying his ascent. ⊗ Contrary to popular belief, **Eli Morgan** is not an investment bank out of the movie *Boiler Room*. Rather, he's a changeup artist who jumped three levels in 2019, striking out more than a batter per inning along the way. ⊗ A rolling stone gathers no moss, but Cleveland picked up **Scott Moss** in the Trevor Bauer trade and he started rocking right afterward. He gave up four runs and accumulated 36 strikeouts in 28 innings with his new organization. ⊗ **Dan Otero** had an arm. O-T-E-R-O. And with that arm he gave up many homers. O-T-E-uh-oh. ⊗ **Luis Oviedo** gave back most of his gains from Mahoning Valley, making his story a relatable one for local gamblers. ⊗ In theory, **Adam Plutko** is a replacement-level pitcher. In practice, he was about two wins below replacement, according to DRA, suggesting any number of random Triple-A pitchers would have performed better. ⊗ If you're going to be a relief prospect, you'd better strike out a ton of batters. Luckily for **Nick Sandlin**, he does just that (36 percent for his career). His spotty command cost him a late-season cup of coffee. ⊗ **Lenny Torres** underwent Tommy John surgery in May. He was the 41st pick in the 2018 draft, so Cleveland has every reason to be patient as he rehabs. ⊗ The crown jewel of Cleveland's 2016 July 2 signing class, **Carlos Vargas** has started filling out his frame and pumping high-90s fastballs. His chance of remaining in a rotation hinges on the development his changeup.

Indians Prospects

The State of the System

It's not a bad system by any means, but it does say something that the first prospect we have a photo of ranks fourth.

The Top Ten

───── ★ ★ ★ *2020 Top 101 Prospect* **#58** ★ ★ ★ ─────

1

George Valera **OF**   OFP: 60   ETA: 2023
Born: 11/13/00   Age: 19   Bats: L   Throws: L   Height: 5'10"   Weight: 160
Origin: International Free Agent, 2017

The Report: There are few in the minor leagues who possess the collection of tools Valera has, and it only takes one look to get a feel for why he's so highly thought of by many in the industry: He has plus hit and power tools thanks to a beautiful, compact swing that delivers hard contact to all fields. The excellent barrel control is a credit to his exceptional balance, as it enables him to make contact with pitches thrown anywhere in the strike zone. He might hit a few too many grounders and still has some pitch recognition kinks to work out, but he nonetheless posted a 132 DRC+ in a league where he was three years younger than the average player: that's special.

While he was listed at 160 pounds for the 2019 season, that admittedly looks rather light (as in, at least 20 pounds light). He has a well-built frame, particularly in the lower half which hasn't impeded his ability to play adequate defense in center, but it could force him into a corner role if he continues to thicken. Still, the fact he earns sufficient defensive grades in center speaks to his athleticism. Should Valera move to a corner spot, he has more than enough bat to profile there.

We want to see how he handles a full season's workload before we full-send on the Valera bandwagon, as his past injuries and load management have sapped him of important reps. Expect him to begin the year with Lake County, where he will once again play against older competition.

Variance: High. Still young, some whiff issues, and non-ideal frame, but he can hit.

Mark Barry's Fantasy Take: The numbers for Valera in 2019 were definitely ugly—he struck out a lot more and generally hit a lot less, neither of which is very encouraging. That said, he'll be 19 years old for the entirety of the 2020 campaign and all of the tools we fell in love with upon his signing are still in the repertoire. Now is the time to see if you can "buy low," as Valera's upside of .290-.300 with decent pop hasn't changed.

———— ★ ★ ★ *2020 Top 101 Prospect* **#66** ★ ★ ★ ————

2

Nolan Jones 3B   OFP: 55   ETA: 2021
Born: 05/07/98   Age: 22   Bats: L   Throws: R   Height: 6'2"   Weight: 185
Origin: Round 2, 2016 Draft (#55 overall)

The Report: The report on Jones remains mostly the same, for good and for ill. It's an unabashed good that he maintained his pop into the upper minors. There's plus-plus raw power, but you are far more likely to see it at 5 p.m, as a lot has to go right for him to get it into games. He will sell out for pull-side pop too often, and the swing gets long and steep, leading to swing-and-miss and a below-average-to-fringe hit tool projection.

That's still enough hit to get 20-odd bombs on the back of the baseball card, but if Jones can refine some things, it might more look like Matt Chapman on the offensive side. It will distinctly not look like Matt Chapman at the hot corner. The arm is plus, but Jones lacks lateral range or great instincts, and although he grinds it out at third, he might be a better fit in an outfield corner as he still runs pretty well. He has enough power for anywhere on the defensive spectrum, but it remains an open question how much the swing and approach will allow it to play in games up the ladder.

Variance: High. It's a good approach, but there's a lot of swing-and-miss in the zone, and he doesn't track breaking balls well. That means the hit tool is going to be high variance, and thus the profile as well.

Mark Barry's Fantasy Take: There are a few too many strikeouts in Jones's arsenal for me to feel really good about paying a premium for him in dynasty leagues. His advanced ability to draw a walk should offset a portion of the strikeout issues, but sitting down to strikes around 30 percent of the time will significantly affect his ability to be even mediocre in the batting average category. He drew a Matt Chapman-upside comp in our Dynasty Midseason 50, but I worry he'll be a less fun 2019 Daniel Vogelbach on the strong side of a platoon.

———— ★ ★ ★ *2020 Top 101 Prospect* **#98** ★ ★ ★ ————

3

Brayan Rocchio SS   OFP: 55   ETA: 2023
Born: 01/13/01   Age: 19   Bats: B   Throws: R   Height: 5'10"   Weight: 150
Origin: International Free Agent, 2017

The Report: Like Valera, Rocchio joined the Indians during the 2017 signing period, although with far less fanfare. Yet he immediately showed signs of being a bargain signing. Despite being joined at the hip by Valera and Aaron Bracho for much of his professional career, his style of play is vastly different. Rocchio displays a plus hit tool from both sides of the plate thanks to a sound approach and really good hand-eye coordination. Hitting for power is not his game, however, as his small frame and average bat speed point to more of a line-drive approach. There is no harm in experimenting with elevating the ball at this point in his development timeline: He began lifting the ball with Mahoning Valley more than he'd done in the past. Even if he fails to make progress in lifting the ball, he has more than enough gap-to-gap power to be effective.

Along with his well-regarded hit tool, Rocchio has the makings of a plus defensive shortstop: He displays good instincts and has no problem going to his left or right. His arm might be the only thing which limits him as a shortstop, though, as it's currently borderline for the position. It's possible the arm improves as he adds much-needed muscle, but as things currently stand there is a non-zero chance he moves to the keystone. To that point, however, he played a handful of games at the position this year and looked rather comfortable, so it should be a seamless transition should it come to that.

Rocchio is not as exciting as some of the other names on this list, yet he still could be a solid ballplayer, one who contributes in a multitude of ways even if there may not be a single standout tool. He earned an aggressive placement in 2019 and likely will do so again in 2020, where he figures to begin the year with Lake County.

Variance: Medium. He is what he is. He just needs more reps and muscle.

Mark Barry's Fantasy Take: This version of Rocchio is the standard "better in real life than in fantasy" dude, blending strong defensive chops with an elite knack for contact at the dish. The good news, for Rocchio and dynasty managers alike, is that he's not a finished product by any stretch, and he has the tools and know-how to develop into a real stolen-base threat while not killing you in power categories. He's super far away, but should still slot into that top-200ish range.

───── ★　★　★ *2020 Top 101 Prospect* **#101** ★　★　★ ─────

4 **James Karinchak　RHP**　　　　　OFP: 60　ETA: 2019
Born: 09/22/95　Age: 24　Bats: R　Throws: R　Height: 6'3"　Weight: 230
Origin: Round 9, 2017 Draft (#282 overall)

The Report: It's hard to describe Karinchak without resorting to complete hyperbole. His fastball and curveball are both true plus-plus offerings bordering on 8s. His strikeout rate went from "very impressive" to "playing The Show on rookie mode" last year, and he continued his dominance in a September cameo.

Karinchak's fastball is a weapon. He throws it at 96-99 from a very tough, extremely high arm slot reminiscent of former major-leaguer Josh Collmenter. It is difficult to pick up, and comes in with plane and life. It's even tougher to jump on because it's paired with Karinchak's curveball, which is frankly just one of the craziest pitches in the minors. It's a power curve, thrown at slider velocity in the mid 80s, but it moves with classic curveball break. The curve just dives out of sight from that high overhand release and leaves batters looking hapless trying to chase it. The two pitches play off each other quite well, and they leave batters looking foolish.

Karinchak does get out of whack mechanically and has walked more batters than you'd like. That was mostly—but not entirely—contained to the period immediately after he came back from a hamstring injury in 2019, and he did tighten his command more broadly year-over-year. But he might still go through wild spells that will give managers fits.

Variance: Medium. Karinchak might already be a very good or great MLB reliever, but he is a reliever with a spotty command history and that profile can be highly variant.

Mark Barry's Fantasy Take: Karinchak debuted in 2019 and got swinging strikes on 16 percent of his pitches. For a full season, that would slot in as one of the top-20 swinging-strike rates in the game, nuzzling up nicely to guys like Kenley Jansen, Kirby Yates, and Will Smith. That will likely be his role in Cleveland too, as a high-strikeout, high-leverage, bullpen arm. It's hard to go crazy for these guys, but Karinchak could be a mainstay in the top-20 relievers as early as 2021.

5   **Daniel Espino   RHP**   OFP: 60   ETA: 2023/24
Born: 01/05/01   Age: 19   Bats: R   Throws: R   Height: 6'2"   Weight: 205
Origin: Round 1, 2019 Draft (#24 overall)

The Report: There were a handful of high schoolers who had a case for best prep arm in the 2019 draft, and Espino was among them. His case rests primarily on the strength of his fastball, which sits mid 90s and routinely touched higher. The pitch showed explosive life and run up in the zone, and he can switch it up to a two-seamer with good sink as well. Espino isn't a pure arm strength play, as he also features two breaking balls with a chance to get to above-average. There's the usual high school pitcher changeup as well. The need for secondary improvements are one of the reasons Espino was merely a candidate for best prep arm and not the consensus pick. He's also fairly close to physically maxed compared to his cohort, and he can struggle with his command and control at times due to a long arm action he doesn't always repeat as well as you'd like. The fastball is good enough that the low minors shouldn't prove much of a challenge. Past there, the offspeed and command developments will determine whether he's a mid-rotation starter or reliever long term.

Variance: High. Espino is a prep pick with a limited pro track record, less projection than usual, and need of secondary development. The usual stuff.

Mark Barry's Fantasy Take: Your mileage may vary on Espino's potential, but it's not difficult to imagine a fantasy SP2 upside for the prep righty. With a heater that flirts with triple digits and three secondaries that flash better than average, perhaps only injuries and control could keep him from hitting that ceiling.

6

Emmanuel Clase   RHP   OFP: 60   ETA: 2019
Born: 03/18/98   Age: 22   Bats: R   Throws: R   Height: 6'2"   Weight: 206
Origin: International Free Agent, 2015

The Report: Emmanuel Clase throws a 100 mph cutter. It's wild. He blitzed High-A and Double-A with the pitch and jumped right to the majors and was a perfectly fine late-inning arm immediately. Brooks Baseball will at times refer to pitches as being "borderline unfair." Well, there's nothing borderline about Clase's fastball. When he's on you have no idea how anyone ever makes contact with it. He pairs it with a pretty good slider as well that sits in the low 90s. If it weren't for the existence of James Karinchak, Clase would be clearly the best pure relief prospect in the minors. Cleveland now has both and hoo boy, is that pen going to be fun to watch for the next few years, health permitting.

Variance: Low. Clase is ready for a late-inning bullpen role now..

Mark Barry's Fantasy Take: If you've ever been on Twitter dot com, you've heard that Clase throws very hard. This is, in fact, true. He'll join Karinchak to form one of the most potent, young bullpen duos in baseball, boasting the skills that will play up in deeper formats or holds leagues. Unfortunately for Clase, he'll need to excel to avoid being relegated to a "Not Corey Kluber" Players Weekend jersey.

7

Logan Allen   LHP   OFP: 55   ETA: 2019
Born: 05/23/97   Age: 23   Bats: R   Throws: L   Height: 6'3"   Weight: 200
Origin: Round 8, 2015 Draft (#231 overall)

The Report: Allen made his major league debut in 2019—winning a one dollar bet with John Cena in the process—but his overall campaign was uneven. Given San Diego's pitching depth, he couldn't really win a rotation spot, and was used a fair bit in long relief. He struggled out of the pen, but the stuff that made him a top 101 prospect remains intact. He got the fastball as high as 97, and the velocity sits a tick above-average from the left side generally. There's a full four-pitch arsenal that he mixes liberally, a good sinking change, a 1-7 breaking ball that's tough on lefties, and an average slider as well. There's nothing here that grades out as plus, which could make him a bit hittable at times in the majors, but there's no real weakness in the repertoire either, as all four pitches are MLB-quality. Cleveland gives him a slightly cleaner shot at a rotation spot, especially if they end up moving Mike Clevinger for some reason, and if he irons out the control and command blips, he remains a high-probability solid stating pitcher.

Variance: Low. Allen had an up-and-down year between Triple-A in the majors across two orgs, and the command issues are a little concerning, but he's a perfectly cromulent 2020 rotation option for Cleveland otherwise.

Mark Barry's Fantasy Take: After being traded to Cleveland, Allen struck out 33 percent of batters faced, walking zero. If he keeps that up, he will be very good. That statline came in just two and a third innings, however, so it might be difficult to rely on that sample. Let's call the lefty a borderline fantasy SP4-5, with upside for a little better if he figures out his command.

8 | **Ethan Hankins   RHP** | OFP: 55   ETA: 2022
Born: 05/23/00   Age: 20   Bats: R   Throws: R   Height: 6'6"   Weight: 200
Origin: Round 1C, 2018 Draft (#35 overall)

The Report: Some might forget that heading into the 2018 draft, Hankins was in consideration for the first overall pick, but a slow spring and some medical issues limited teams' interest. Despite that, he began 2019 with an aggressive assignment to Mahoning Valley and had some success before receiving an even-more-aggressive promotion to Lake County. I wrote up Hankins after one of his starts against Staten Island, where he displayed some fire-breathing stuff: The fastball was 94-97 with late life, the curve broke late and tunneled real well with the heater, and the slider was a distant yet sufficient third pitch. He has seldom used his changeup, though it's shown enough tumbling action for us to consider it another legitimate pitch in the repertoire.

Despite this impressive arsenal, there are some red flags we can't ignore. Most notably, Hankins started losing velocity on his heater and command of his secondaries once he got into the third inning of his outings. We believe this is the result of his cross-body throwing motion: Such arm action has been known to cause inconsistent release points that lead to decreased velocity and diminished command over the course of an appearance. This, in combination with his suspect injury history, leads some to believe he might be a future reliever (albeit a darn good one).

But like many of the prospects on this list, Hankins has enjoyed some success against older competition, and another year removed from injuries could help him unleash his obvious talent on a more consistent basis. We'd be remiss to not point out that Cleveland is one of the best at extracting max value from pitchers like this, so Hankins is in an ideal development spot. The educated guess is he starts in Lake County, though don't count out the club aggressively assigning him to Lynchburg.

Variance: Extreme. The mechanics and injury history are worrisome.

Mark Barry's Fantasy Take: A classic "High Ceiling/Low Floor" guy, Hankins's profile is awfully similar to Espino's, and dips slightly thanks to more recent injury woes. If he can stay healthy, and in turn throw more strikes, he could be a top-25 starter. He's a long way away from both, however.

9 **Daniel Johnson OF**   OFP: 50 ETA: 2020
Born: 07/11/95   Age: 24   Bats: L   Throws: L   Height: 5'10"   Weight: 200
Origin: Round 5, 2016 Draft (#154 overall)

The Report: Johnson remains equal parts tantalizing and frustrating as an outfield prospect. He made some adjustments to Double-A in his second try, and continued to hit for solid power with the Triple-A baseball. He's always had impressive pound-for-pound raw power, but has tended to be limited in terms of how much he gets it into games due to a violent uppercut and his free-swinging ways. When we were watching his Futures Game batting practice, Chris Blessing noted to me that his swing is more or less perfect for depositing balls about five rows deep in the right field stands at Progessive Field, so if he can tame his approach some, he could pop 20+ home runs in the bigs. Johnson has thickened up some and slowed down and now splits his time between center field and right. He has one of the best outfield arms in the minors, and can handle any of the three outfield spots. The variance here remains sneakily high for a prospect about ready for the majors, but if Johnson can hit .250 or so, he'll be a useful major leaguer for a good while.

Variance: Medium. Hit tool questions remain even after a strong upper minors performance, but Johnson's pop and ability to handle all three outfield spots give him a reasonably safe bench outfielder floor.

Mark Barry's Fantasy Take: In another organization, Johnson might be destined for a role as a platoon bat at best, never getting a chance to develop with regular reps. Luckily for Johnson, Cleveland has roughly 1.5 viable, big-league outfielders, so he should get plenty of opportunities to prove his worth. If his plate discipline improvements from 2019 are real, he should stick as a fantasy OF5.

10 **Bo Naylor C**   OFP: 50 ETA: 2022
Born: 02/21/00   Age: 20   Bats: L   Throws: R   Height: 6'0"   Weight: 195
Origin: Round 1, 2018 Draft (#29 overall)

The Report: Nabbed by the Indians at the end of the first round in 2018, Naylor held his own in his first full season assignment. As one of the youngest position players in the Midwest League he struggled offensively in the early cold weather but seemed to find his stroke as the season warmed. He's a tough out from the left side with innate bat to ball skills and a good knowledge of the strike zone. There's still room in the frame for good weight to be added as he matures. That added strength and his existing bat speed will get the pop to eventually play as average in-game. Defensively, he will get every opportunity to remain behind the plate but will eventually land elsewhere on the diamond. Athletic and nimble, he moves well showing the ability to block pitches in the dirt. However, the arm strength is lacking and can be a liability against speedy teams.

Variance: High. It's likely Naylor ends up somewhere on the right side of the infield. That's going to put a ton of pressure on the bat to continue to develop.

Mark Barry's Fantasy Take: As far as catching prospects go, I kinda/sorta like Naylor. He spent his age-19 season in full-season ball, which portends well to him sticking behind the dish. If he does, Naylor could be a top-10 catcher. If he doesn't, he'll still be useful-ish as a .260ish guy with 20-25 homers.

The Next Ten

11   **Triston McKenzie   RHP**
Born: 08/02/97   Age: 22   Bats: R   Throws: R   Height: 6'5"   Weight: 165
Origin: Round 1, 2015 Draft (#42 overall)

Two years ago, McKenzie threw 143 innings as a 19-year-old, so despite the string bean physique, he'd shown a fair amount of durability for a pitching prospect. Since then, he missed the first few months of 2018 with a forearm issue, and then all of 2019 with a back issue. Pitchers, man. So a mere 24 months later we have a 21-year-old string bean who hasn't shown he can really handle the rigors of pitching once every 5-6 days. Now, he will be just 22 in 2020, and with experience in Double-A. We know the fastball/curve combo is already major-league quality, assuming it's still there next time he steps on the mound. As for where to rank McKenzie? Well, that we were less sure of. There's an argument he's still the best pitching prospect in this system, but ontologically speaking, you have to pitch to be a pitching prospect.

12   **Tyler Freeman   SS**
Born: 05/21/99   Age: 21   Bats: R   Throws: R   Height: 6'0"   Weight: 170
Origin: Round 2, 2017 Draft (#71 overall)

Occasionally my aesthetic preferences will lead me astray. I haven't been a huge fan of Freeman's swing. It isn't merely art, though, there's some science, as it uses a bunch of timing mechanisms including a double toe tap. But look, it works. Kid can hit. He's compact once he gets going with good barrel control, although given his lack of physicality and loft, power is never going to be a big part of the game. That limits the upside, but he can hit a bit, run a bit, and play a passable shortstop. That's potentially a solid major leaguer. I'm a stubborn Italian though, so I still want to see how he does in Double-A first before I sign off on his being in the top 10 in an improving Cleveland system.

13   **Sam Hentges   LHP**
Born: 07/18/96   Age: 23   Bats: L   Throws: L   Height: 6'8"   Weight: 245
Origin: Round 4, 2014 Draft (#128 overall)

Ordinarily speaking, dropping from fifth to 13th is pretty significant, but it overstates how badly Hentges' 2019 went in Double-A. It was a rough transition to be sure, and he struggled to throw enough good strikes—or even strikes generally—with his mid-90s fastball, but it is a mid-90s fastball from the left side. We can work with that. Hentges added a cutter in 2018 and it gives him a wrinkle to get inside against righties as his fastball can run a little true. He has good feel for the curveball, although it could lack depth at times and get a little sweepy from his three-quarters slot. The command and control need to get tightened up to avoid a future bullpen role, but the needle hasn't moved down that much on Hentges this year—there's a bit more relief risk, but still No. 4 starter OFP—it's more a matter of an improving system around him.

14 **Aaron Bracho   2B**
Born: 04/24/01   Age: 19   Bats: B   Throws: R   Height: 5'11"   Weight: 175
Origin: International Free Agent, 2017

Bracho got a larger bonus than Valera and Rocchio combined, netting $1.5 million when he signed out of Venezuela in 2017. Like Rocchio, he is a switch-hitting middle infielder with more polish than projection. Unlike Rocchio he is already playing almost exclusively second base. The frame and swing remind me a bit of Andrés Giménez at the same age, although Bracho is a bit stouter and less quick-twitch. That could portend more power down the line, but Bracho may lack a carrying tool, and as a second baseman there's less upside and floor. Then again, the 18-year-old version of Giménez went in a slightly different direction than I expected, and Bracho can really hit. There's a shot for a solid regular here, but we'll need to see him out of the complex first.

15 **Luis Oviedo   RHP**
Born: 05/15/99   Age: 21   Bats: R   Throws: R   Height: 6'4"   Weight: 170
Origin: International Free Agent, 2015

We stuck Oviedo at the back of last year's 101 on the strength of his mid-90s fastball and rapidly-developing slider. He promptly came out in 2019 in full-season ball sitting a little over 90 and with the slider looking a bit slurvy. Pitchers, man. It's not uncommon for pop-up velocity guys—Oviedo was a little below 90 mph when he signed—to give back the velocity in subsequent years, but it's still disappointing. Oviedo has a nearly ideal starting pitcher's frame, a well-proportioned 6-foot-4, and a fairly simple, repeatable delivery. Fastball velocity isn't everything, mind you, but the rest of the package isn't going to carry low-90s heat. On what he showed in 2019, this ranking would be too high, but we know a plus fastball is in there somewhere. And Oviedo won't turn 21 until six weeks into the 2020 season, so we can hope the stuff returns. Wait 'til next year, I guess.

16 **Yu Chang   IF**
Born: 08/18/95   Age: 24   Bats: R   Throws: R   Height: 6'1"   Weight: 180
Origin: International Free Agent, 2013

You know what you are getting from Chang at this point—medium pop from a fairly long swing, the ability to play multiple infield positions, sneaky speed, and a below-average hit tool, due to the aforementioned length. It likely doesn't all add up to a major league starter, especially given—well, at the time of publication—Cleveland's infield depth. But there's value in a right-handed bat with pop that can handle second, third, and short. If one of your starters has to miss a month, Chang will keep you above water. It's not sexy, but it's a major leaguer. Well…probably. His first pass against major league pitching exposed some issues with the swing, and it's a fine line between hitting .240 or .250 with enough pop to be useful, and hitting .220 and having to shell out for a bunch of $100 Uber rides from Columbus to Cleveland.

17 **Will Benson   OF**
Born: 06/16/98   Age: 22   Bats: L   Throws: L   Height: 6'5"   Weight: 225
Origin: Round 1, 2016 Draft (#14 overall)

It's a cliche to say we are not selling jeans here. It's even a cliche now to turn that around and suggest that Benson could definitely sell a pair of Levi's 501s. He has a physique equal parts hulking and athletic. Even stooped over some at the plate, he dwarfs most everyone else in A-ball. The raw power is top of the scale, and he's worth getting to the park early to see take a batting practice session when he's in town. In addition to being built like an NFL wideout, he runs like one, too. Unfortunately, the swing-and-miss remains a major impediment to getting the raw power into games. Benson has long levers and struggles when he can't hunt a fastball. Despite his speed, the defensive profile works better in a corner. He adjusted second time through the Midwest League, but once again ended up on the interstate post-promotion to the Carolina League. You have to always keep an eye on him given the physical tools here, but three years since he was drafted in the first round, the performance just hasn't been there.

18 **Lenny Torres   RHP**
Born: 10/15/00   Age: 19   Bats: R   Throws: R   Height: 6'1"   Weight: 190
Origin: Round 1, 2018 Draft (#41 overall)

Last year I said I would have had Torres ahead of Ethan Hankins on a personal pref list because he hadn't had a bout of shoulder soreness yet. Sorry about that, Cleveland fans. Torres had Tommy John surgery last May and will likely not see a mound again until the middle of next season at the earliest. He was a raw, cold-weather prep arm coming out of the 2018 draft, so the lost development time hurts even more and will only amplify the relief risk in the profile. We may not have a good feel for what Torres is until well into 2021 at this point, but there was a potential plus fastball/slider combo here this time last year.

19

Oscar Gonzalez   OF
Born: 01/10/98   Age: 22   Bats: R   Throws: R   Height: 6'2"   Weight: 180
Origin: International Free Agent, 2014

With his strengths and weaknesses, González is an entertaining prospect whose ultimate destination is difficult to pin down. He's a natural hitter who uses his excellent hand-eye coordination and feel for the barrel to square up pitches of all types and locations, or deploys his long arms to foul them away if they're not quite to his liking. He also doesn't have an approach. Not only does he not draw walks, he can seem loath to take a pitch at all. This tendency could create a lot of weak contact as he jumps levels and is faced with pitchers possessed of better command. It also lowers his ultimate ceiling; more selectivity would give him a better chance to tap into his above-average raw power. His defense should be fine, but he's already marooned in the less glamorous corner. Let's see how he hits in Double-A.

20

Nick Sandlin   RHP
Born: 01/10/97   Age: 23   Bats: R   Throws: R   Height: 5'11"   Weight: 175
Origin: Round 2, 2018 Draft (#67 overall)

Sandlin could give the 2020 Cleveland bullpen quite the three-headed monster along with Karinchak and Clase, health permitting. The 2018 second-round pick continued to miss bats in the upper minors with his low-90s fastball/low-80s slider combo from a deceptive sidearm slot. The fastball sinks and runs, and the slider tunnels well in the opposite direction. The funk can lead to bouts of wildness, but he's a tough at-bat, especially for righties. "Health permitting" is doing a lot of heavy lifting though, as he got a late start to his season while dealing with a forearm issue that ended up as a strain in late June, ending his season early. A healthy Sandlin has setup arm potential, so check back in a month or so.

Personal Cheeseball

Bobby Bradley   1B/DH
Born: 05/29/96   Age: 24   Bats: L   Throws: R   Height: 6'1"   Weight: 225
Origin: Round 3, 2014 Draft (#97 overall)

Bradley's major-league OPS barely topped his Triple-A slugging in 2019, so the Quad-A warning light has begun to blink brighter now. He struggled mightily against offspeed moving down and/or away from him—a recurring theme throughout his pro career—and his stiff, leveraged swing really needs fastballs up and out over the plate. When he gets one…well go look up the video of his first major league home run. Despite 70 raw power, he's not going to see enough of those to carry a DH profile, and the OFP now might be "2022 KBO home run champ," but until then you can rest assured Bradley will never get cheated in any MLB at-bat to come.

Low Minors Sleeper

LMS **Jose Fermin   SS**
Born: 03/29/99   Age: 21   Bats: R   Throws: R   Height: 5'11"   Weight: 160
Origin: International Free Agent, 2015

Fermin was a multiple-time entrant in the "What Scouts are Saying" column this year, and it's no surprise he got plaudits from the area guys. He's exactly the type of prospect who endears himself quickly. He's a plus runner in the middle infield, smooth and sure-handed, although the arm is a better fit for second than short. At the plate he has a good eye and good plate coverage, in part due to a big leg kick that lets him dive for the outside pitch. He's still quick enough inside to pull base hits when you try to beat him there, and there's a bit of sneaky pop in there too, although it's likely to play mostly for doubles. Fermin is the kind of guy you gush about behind the plate and then write up as a 40 or a 45, but hey, that's a major league grade.

Top Talents 25 and Under (as of 4/1/2020)

1. Shane Bieber
2. Franmil Reyes
3. Oscar Mercado
4. George Valera
5. Nolan Jones
6. Brayan Rocchio
7. James Karinchak
8. Daniel Espino
9. Jake Bauers
10. Emmanuel Clase

It really wasn't very long ago that the Indians played extra innings in Game 7 of the World Series. Even more recently, they seemingly had a stranglehold on the American League Central, without a legit challenger in sight. A lacking sense of urgency led to a handful of consecutive complacent offseasons, culminating last year, with a $2.5 million renewal of the ageless wonder Oliver Perez serving as their crowning achievement in free agency. Since that World Series, the team payroll has dropped precipitously, currently checking in as the 25th highest in the league—cool for the bottom line, but less enticing for a team with "serious" championship aspirations.

The payroll purge continued into this offseason, with veteran-ace Corey Kluber jettisoned for a reliever and fourth outfielder while Mike Clevinger and Francisco Lindor have both been hot names on the trade market. You could even rationalize a Clevinger move in a vacuum—he's older than you think and despite gaudy strikeout numbers, he has been recently banged up. Trading Lindor would be the ultimate betrayal. Not only is he one of the five-ish best players in the league, he's a guy who's super easy to root for in a sports landscape that doesn't always churn out likable dudes. Sure the haul would be sizable, but there's really only one reason why you would trade a 26-year-old franchise cornerstone and it doesn't have much to do with competing for postseason success (at least the fans will see tickets and concessions become more affordable—wait…).

Even though things seem less than ideal in the organization, and the Twins (and maybe the White Sox) have cruised past the Indians in their competitive cycle, there are still some positives to build upon. As of this writing, Lindor is still on the team, and he'll remain one-half of baseball's best left side with Jose Ramirez, who after a truly puzzling stretch at the plate, slashed .327/.365/.739 in the second half before a broken hamate bone ended his season. Even without Kluber and the dearly departed Trevor Bauer, the Tribe's rotation is still formidable with U25 star and newly-minted staff ace Shane Bieber seeking to build on his first 200+ inning campaign. After a season spent fighting Leukemia, Carlos Carrasco slots in nicely as a No. 3 starter, providing rotation stability in addition to a ridiculously good story that is super easy to root for. And while most people rolled their eyes at the Kluber return, tossing Clase into a bullpen that already features Karinchak and Brad Hand, late-inning relief in Cleveland should be awfully fun to watch.

On the farm, there isn't a ton of immediate help on the way. Johnson should see some time in the big-league outfield, and there's an outside chance Jones could make an appearance if he cleans up a few of his strikeout tendencies. Even though proximity might not be one of the standout characteristics of most Cleveland prospects, the system is super deep with dudes who could provide solid production with the big club. The organization is oozing with talented middle-infield prospects with strong hit tools, led by Rocchio, with guys like Aaron Bracho, Tyler Freeman and Gabriel Rodriguez not far behind. And speaking of hit tools, Valera and Bo Naylor could both be plus hitters up the middle. Based on how Cleveland has been able to develop pitchers over the last handful of seasons, it seems unfair that both Espino and Ethan Hankins are in this organization, as both could mature to be frontline starters. There are a lot of "could be" and "potential to"s in this organization, and with some development, this system could float through org ranks with a Padres-like speed. Hopefully some of these young studs get the opportunity to play with Lindor.

Part 3: Featured Articles

The Baseball Is Juiced (Again)

Robert Arthur

This article originally appeared at Baseball Prospectus on April 5, 2019.

It started when the normally reliable Chris Sale got lit up for three homers by the Mariners in the Red Sox's season opener. It was part of a record number of taters that flew on Opening Day, as starters from Sale to Zack Greinke were taken deep by the handful. Then Christian Yelich hit a home run in each of his first four games, tying yet another MLB record, this one for consecutive games with a dinger to start a season.

It didn't take long for fans and players to begin whispering and tweeting about the baseballs being juiced again. It's early yet for us to come to any definitive conclusion about the 2019 season, but preliminary data shows that the baseball has returned to its aerodynamic peak. Whether that means this season will smash home run records like 2017 did remains to be seen.

Before home run explosion over the last few years, no one worried too much about the baseball's air resistance. While MLB and Rawlings (the company that manufactures the official baseballs) kept track of dozens of metrics to make sure that the ball was consistent from month to month, they didn't measure drag.

But drag is incredibly important in determining how likely a hitter is to knock one out of the park. As baseballs become more aerodynamic, they travel further given a certain initial velocity. A deep fly ball that might have been caught at the warning track can instead go into the first row of the stands. A three percent change in drag coefficient can work to add about five feet to a well-hit fly ball, which can in turn increase home runs league wide by an astounding 10-15 percent.

It's possible to measure the aerodynamics of the baseball using the pitch-tracking radars currently in place in each MLB ballpark. By calculating the loss of speed from when the pitch is released to when it crosses the plate, you can directly measure the drag coefficient on the baseball. I first wrote about the role of decreasing drag in boosting home runs in 2017, and MLB's commission of scientists and statisticians later confirmed that the more aerodynamic baseballs in use that year were largely to blame for the spike in home runs. The same commission rejected some alternate hypotheses, like rising temperatures and a league-wide boost in launch angle pushing more balls over the fence.

The current era has featured some large fluctuations in drag coefficient, leading to first an explosion in 2016 and 2017, and then a dialing back of homers last year. Curious about the record-breaking home run tallies in the last few days, I used the same methodology to measure the aerodynamics of the baseballs so far in 2019.

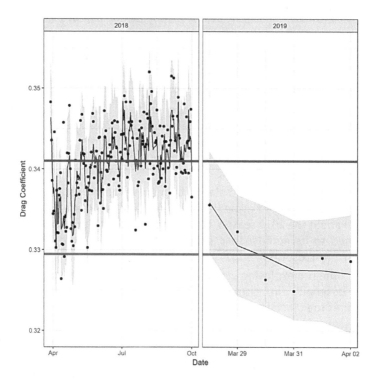

We're only a week into the 2019 season, but the drag numbers so far are among the lowest recorded in the last calendar year. With apologies for gory math, the current 2019 season average drag coefficient (the red line) would be below the 95 percent credible interval (the shaded area) for about nine-tenths of the 2018 season. (I used a Bayesian Random Walk model implemented in INLA to calculate these credible intervals, averaging the drag numbers in each game and adjusting for park.)

There were only a handful of six-day stretches in 2018 that had drag numbers below what we're seeing now, and most were in late June and early July. All of this means that 2019's data so far is quite a bit different than what we saw through most of last year.

These drag coefficients factor out the effects of temperature and air density, so they aren't a product of April cold. However, the numbers could be deceptive if the radars used to track pitches have changed from year to year. I consulted with some experts within baseball who were not aware of any specific modifications to the radar this year that could produce this pattern, but it's an important caveat of which to be aware.

On the one hand, it's only been six days, and we don't quite have the statistical basis to say that these drag coefficients are unprecedented compared to 2018. On the other hand, we've witnessed about 5,000 fastballs so far this season, so it's not as if our sample size is small. At least so far, the baseball has played like it's much more aerodynamic than it was last year. In fact, the current drag coefficient is really only comparable to 2017, when the baseballs were more aerodynamic than they had been in at least a decade.

It's not just fancy radar tracking indicating that the baseball is flying through the air more easily. The current number of home runs per game (as of this writing) is the highest it's been since the heady days of 2017, the year that teams and players broke dinger-related records everywhere you looked. That's especially remarkable considering that we're in what is typically the coldest part of the regular season, when lower temperatures and higher winds tend to suppress offense and keep balls in the air within the park. Comparing only from April to April, this year's rate of home runs per fly ball is even a little bit higher than it was in 2017.

With that said, the current measurements are no guarantee that 2019 will be another year of record-shattering homer hitting. The trouble with the drag measurements is that they are not consistent from June to August, from week to week, or even sometimes from day to day. Whether because of natural manufacturing variation or differences in the underlying supplies of cowhide and thread that go into the baseballs, drag has a tendency to fluctuate up and down over the course of a year. So the homers that fly in the first week of April wouldn't necessarily clear the fence a week later.

It's possible that this one-week drop in drag coefficient subsides and the baseball returns to its 2018 levels. On the other hand, it's almost equally probable that the ball becomes even more slippery and flies ever farther. Either way, it's clear that the baseball's air resistance is something to keep an eye on for the remainder of the 2019 season.

—*Robert Arthur is an author of Baseball Prospectus.*

The Moral Hazard of Playing It Safe

Craig Goldstein

This article originally appeared at Baseball Prospectus on August 6, 2019.

A couple days prior to the trade deadline, amidst a sea of tranquility posing as the lead up to the trade deadline, Bob Nightengale took to Twitter. Nightengale, who was probably wearing his pants backwards at the time, tweeted that MLB GMs were coming around on the idea that the unified trade deadline should be moved back from July 31 to August 15, so they could better assess their positions in the standings and whether they should buy or sell. To which I said:

This might strike some as reductive and churlish. And it might be that, but it isn't really wrong, either. Jeff Quinton wrote a great piece discussing the environmental factors that enable front offices to avoid risk without upsetting the apple cart within their own fanbases. I don't believe that it goes far enough, however. His article gives us the proper framework through which to understand why these behaviors have been allowed to seep into front offices throughout the league. Understanding the reasons behind these actions are different from excusing them, though, and GMs should not be let off the hook for their non-competitive approach to the trade deadline (much less the offseason).

⚾   ⚾   ⚾

It's fair to say that fans as a group have rarely, if ever, been pro-player. It is also fair to say that in the time during and following the Moneyball revolution, the pendulum swung from fans who cared intensely about winning in the moment (and thus might be intolerant of a rebuilding approach) to fans who supported building a team that could compete throughout multiple seasons, viewing the playoffs as a crapshoot, with the thought that getting multiple bites at the apple was a better approach than taking a bigger bite in any one season.

There's nothing wrong with that approach, and I still find merit in that argument. However, it seems that the pendulum has swung too far in that direction. Teams are overvaluing some of the individual factors that make themselves long-term contenders rather than attempting to seize a championship when given the opportunity. It's a difficult needle to thread.

And surely, they (and those in similar positions) would have liked another two weeks to clarify where they stand so as to better marshal their resources. We've all asked for a few more minutes when staring at a menu. But all of these GMs and front office personnel are where they are to make difficult decisions. They have proprietary data and internal analysts dedicated to understanding their position relative to the rest of the league, and how any move in the here and now impacts their long-term vision. To complain (if that report is accurate) that over half the season is not enough to properly assess their season is bullshit of the highest order. Move the deadline, and you'd simply have increasingly discounted trade offers because teams would be acquiring even less control of anyone they're acquiring, rental or not.

Major league front offices are behaving like the managers they lampooned two decades ago. They're effectively sacrificing a runner to second in the ninth inning—not because it's the correct move, but rather because it is safe. It used to be that the phrase "moral hazard" was used to describe general managers who made ill-fated, short-sighted decisions aimed at locking in wins and securing their jobs at the expense of their team's future. Now, general managers are guilty of committing moral hazards in the opposite direction, playing it utterly safe and terrified of becoming scapegoats.

In lieu of bold action, they opt to pussyfoot around a current window of contention, choosing instead to play the long game and stack up years of control like they're blocks in a game of Jenga. GMs pass on signing quality players in free agency because the back-end of the deal might look bad, and because they might be able to squeeze out 70 percent of the production from a player who costs a tenth as much. That's a safer investment, too, because it's also hard to prove a negative—it's impossible to prove that Manny Machado would make the Mets a playoff team in 2019-2020, but it's easy to say that the back half of Robinson Cano's contract sucks. Owners, who rule over GM's jobs, are also humans with human brain processes that will always make the so-called albatross contract uglier than the road not taken.

These days, GMs are remembered for the bad deals they make and the surplus value they generate, not the acquisition of expensive, necessary talents that meet their market worth (or fall slightly short while still providing significant on-field value). And front offices know that one or two expensive misfires can cost them their jobs, no matter how many good deals they make.

No front office exemplifies this ethos more than the Toronto Blue Jays. General Manager Ross Atkins had this to say following the Blue Jays underwhelming trade deadline:

Scott Stinson ✔
@scott_stinson

On a conference call, Jays GM Ross Atkins says the team's moves have 'turned 14 years of control into 42 years of control'.

gonna be tough for the marketing folks to work that into a slogan.

♡ 894   1:26 PM - Jul 31, 2019   ⓘ

💬 346 people are talking about this   ›

This is by no means the first time that an executive will cite years of control to justify their actions, which is often just another way of saying "don't look at what we got, look at how much we got of it." Atkins touts quantity to elide the discussion of quality—either, that of the players acquired, or those given up. Remember: the other teams presumably value years of control, too.

Atkins also had some thoughts to offer regarding free agents back in early 2018:

> **Pitch Talks** ✔
> @PitchTalks
>
> #BlueJays GM Ross Atkins "when you're talking about free agency you're talking about aging players and the trend of overpaying a player's aging curves has come to an end across baseball"
>
> ♡ 62   6:09 PM · Feb 1, 2018 · The Rivoli
>
> ○ 59 people are talking about this

This ignores, of course, whether the player can create enough value in the front end of a contract to justify the longer term of a deal, and the decline that often occurs in the back end. It also ignores whether the player can fill a need the team requires and put them in a position to compete for and win a championship. But as teams seemingly avoid contention at all, where they might end up having to consider and later justify some of these tough decisions, we still see risk-averse approaches.

Anthony Fenech's article on two trades that recently extended GM Al Avila didn't make got at this issue rather well:

> Passing on those deals was defensible: Both players had yet to break out and trading [Michael] Fulmer—a pitcher who appeared to be a future ace, no matter his injury concerns—would have taken serious gumption, opening Avila up to strong criticism.

Avoiding strong criticism is something each of us can understand as a motivation, but the avoidance of criticism only matters if that criticism is valid. In Fulmer's case, shoving his injury concerns aside affects not only the years that the team controls him (he is currently missing a full season due to Tommy John surgery) but also the quality of those seasons, as his knee and elbow injuries combined to dampen his effectiveness even when healthy enough to pitch. But it was easy to present the then-current image of Fulmer as a top of the rotation pitcher who the team had under its domain for the next five seasons as something to build around. The status quo isn't nearly as often second-guessed as a decision that disrupts it.

⚾   ⚾   ⚾

MLB GMs are risk-averse to a fault. They are ivy-educated and consulting firm-approved, and yet they can't seem to avoid leaving wins on the table in their all-consuming lust for a non-existent $/WAR championship. They are supposed to zig when everyone else zags, and not merely pay lip service to the idea of zigging through a calculated PR plan built on convincing the fan base their approach is novel when it actually apes most of their competitors. Instead they've become far more concerned with making safe, accepted-by-the-new-common-wisdom decisions, such that our prior understanding of what a moral hazard is has become inverted.

I can't blame them entirely, and not only because of the reasons that Quinton illuminated in his article, but also because of the damage wrought by the introduction of the second wild card (WC2) spot. MLB's desire to have more teams in playoff contention has sparked anti-competitive behavior. Teams know now that they do not need to swing big as they assemble their roster because there is a good chance that a mediocre team can either catch fire and capture a division, or muddle along until they back into the WC2.

Simultaneously, the one-game playoff has neutered the WC1, putting an entire season on the flip of a coin like some sort of baseball-obsessed Anton Chigurh. While the one-game playoff makes sense as a way to increase the value of winning a division, it also means that if a front office doesn't like its chances of overcoming a behemoth like the Dodgers or Astros in the offseason, they have few incentives to chase glory. Similarly, the relative inaction in the NL Central at the trade deadline—despite a wide open division—can be explained by the idea that any high-variance investment could still result in only a wild card (or worse) result, given the mere two months left in the season to make an impact.

⚾   ⚾   ⚾

As stated at the top, we should not confuse reasons for excuses. The implementation of the second wild card is just one of many environmental factors that influence how each front office operates. I am convinced that it is one of the larger factors, but I am also convinced that organizations need to shed the yoke of "efficiency at all costs" so that they can instead pursue competition, as the spirit of the game intends. Until they do, we're all deadline losers.

—Craig Goldstein is an author of Baseball Prospectus.

Index of Names

Cleveland Indians 2020